Business Letters Ready to Go!

Anne Basye

NTC Business Books

Library of Congress Cataloging-in-Publication Data

Basye, Anne.
    Business letters ready to go! / Anne Basye.
        p.   cm.
    ISBN 0-8442-3571-7
        1. Commercial correspondence—Handbooks, manuals, etc.
    2. Letter writing—Handbooks, manuals, etc. 3. Form letters.
    I. Title.
    HF5726.B29   1998
    651.7′5—dc21   98-9247
                                                                CIP

Cover design by Nick Panos
Interior design by City Desktop Productions, Inc.

Portions of this book were previously published as *Credit and Collection Letters Ready to Go!*, *Everyday Letters Ready to Go!*, *Sales Letters Ready to Go!*, *Personnel Letters Ready to Go!*, and *Customer Service Letters Ready to Go!*

Published by NTC Business Books
A division of NTC/Contemporary Publishing Group, Inc.
4255 West Touhy Avenue, Lincolnwood (Chicago), Illinois 60646-1975 U.S.A.
Copyright © 1998 by NTC/Contemporary Publishing Group, Inc.
Printed in the United States of America
International Standard Book Number: 0-8442-3571-7

18 17 16 15 14 13 12 11 10 9 8 7 6 5 4 3 2 1

Contents

The Basics of Good Business Writing

People in business, whatever their place on the organizational chart, spend a good part of each day exchanging information: calling vendors, presenting to superiors, trading gossip with peers, or writing and calling customers.

Whenever there is an exchange, there is also the chance for misunderstanding and the transmittal of incorrect information. Miscommunication is costly to business. It means wasted time and wasted dollars. People who can express themselves well, both verbally and in writing, are sought after and highly prized. This one skill, the ability to communicate effectively, may well be the difference between business success and business failure—both for the individual and the organization.

The purpose of this book is to help you master one aspect of your communication responsibilities: letter writing. Writing by its very nature is difficult. Trying to string words together so they are clear and say what you mean is a true challenge. It can also be as backbreaking as working construction. No wonder otherwise competent people try to avoid the task altogether!

Contrary to popular belief, good writers aren't blessed by the Muses. They simply practice enough until it seems as if they are. Writing well can be learned. Good business writing, like anything else, doesn't simply "happen." It isn't a matter of luck or chance but is based on something far less elusive and abstract: planning.

Strategy for Effective Written Communication

When it comes to creating effective letters, planning is as important as the actual writing. Long before a single word is written you should have a road map that shows how to get from point A to point B. The following six steps constitute a strategy that can be applied to any letter, no matter how long.

Step 1: Determine Your Objectives

The first step in preparing for your writing trip is to decide what you want to accomplish. What exactly is your goal or desired outcome? Are you writing to inform? To explain? To persuade? To request materials or a specific action?

Though your message may have one primary objective, it is likely it will also have one or more secondary purposes. It may help you focus your writing if you try to state in one sentence the purpose of your communication. Begin by listing the key goal first, followed by any other intentions of lesser significance.

Step 2: Understand Your Reader

Who is your reader? You will certainly have a greater chance for communication success if you know who you are writing to. Your audience will determine the content of your message, the approach used, and even the tone of the message. An accountant, for example, could use terminology in a report to another accountant that he or she couldn't use in writing to someone who doesn't have a financial background. To such a person GAAP (generally accepted accounting principles) may mean nothing more than a place to buy jeans.

Knowing your reader allows you to tailor your message for maximum impact and understandability. Here are some general guidelines you may follow to make sure your messages are appropriate for your audience:

- Write to the knowledge level of your readers. If they are not technical types, avoid jargon, acronyms, and other "alphabet soup" that will get in the way of your meaning.

- Decide how much detail is needed. If you are writing the 99th memo on a subject, it shouldn't be necessary to recap everything that has happened since memo number one.

- Personalize your writing so each reader feels you are speaking directly to him or her. Be professional, yet cordial.

- Write from the readers' perspective. Show why your message should interest them or how they will benefit by following your recommendations.

- Avoid language that could be interpreted as sexist, racist, or in other ways discriminatory. It is unlikely that readers offended by your message will respond at all, let alone do anything you have asked.

KNOW YOUR READER

In order to write an effective letter, you need to know who you're writing to and how that knowledge might affect what you're going to write. Start by asking yourself the following questions about your reader:

- What questions or concerns does the reader have?

- How does the reader feel about your company (product, service)?

- How much influence does the customer have on future sales? (Is this a buyer for a major corporation? Will a mistake risk the customer's goodwill—or your position?)

- If you are responding to a customer, what is the customer's general mood—angry? dissatisfied? satisfied? questioning? friendly? indifferent?

- What are the reader's expectations? Why will the reader be interested in your letter?

- What does the reader already know about this situation?

- How will the reader use the information you present?

- What tone and style will be most effective in reaching this customer?

- How do you want the reader to feel after reading your letter?

When you have answered these questions, put yourself in the position of your customer. What kind of letter would you expect to receive? What information would persuade you to take the action you desire from your customer?

Step 3: Collect the Facts

Once you have outlined your objectives and evaluated your audience, collect the information needed to make your message complete and factually correct. If you are making a recommendation to a committee, for example, you should include data that supports the course of action you are suggesting. Resolving a complaint that has been ongoing for months might involve reviewing any notes or earlier correspondence on the subject, or speaking with individuals familiar with the matter to pinpoint specific obstacles to resolution.

While you're gathering facts, you should also be brainstorming about what will go in your letter. Jot down ideas as they come to you. Build on the objective lists you began at the start of the assignment. Write down what you want to get across, perhaps even putting down key phrases you wish to include in your correspondence. Outline all the points you want to be sure to cover. Try to foresee objections so you can counter them in your message. All this preliminary work will pay off when you begin to write.

Step 4: Set the Right Tone

Every letter has a tone that communicates more loudly than the words themselves. Letters from companies often sound so formal and stuffy that the reader doesn't wade through the verbiage. It's also possible to be too flippant or cute in a letter and appear as ungracious or offensive.

One word defines the overall tone of every good letter: *respectful.* Whether you want to be firm or friendly, formal or casual, your letter should always be respectful, courteous, and reasonable. Put yourself in the place of the reader who receives the following:

Dear Ms. Wilson:

I received your letter, but I couldn't see what you had to complain about with the service at Dino-Dips. Our servers are kept very busy and have more important things to do than heat baby bottles. You should be responsible for such special individual requirements as we can't possibly anticipate your every need.

Respectfully,

Jane Doe
Customer Service Associate

Closing with "respectfully" does nothing to mitigate the damage done by the disrespectful tone of the letter itself. It communicates that the customer's concern is considered stupid and the customer herself is thought frivolous and of little value to the letter writer.

This example also lacks another message your tone should convey: *appreciation*. Let your customer know you appreciate hearing concerns and problems as well as compliments—even when you're writing bad news.

Your tone will depend in large measure on whether you're writing good news, bad news, or routine information. A letter bearing only good news can adopt a positive, informal, and friendly tone. To set an informal, friendly tone:

- Use *I* and *you.*

- Write as if you were conversing directly with your reader.

- Use contractions such as *you're, it's, I'm, we're, isn't.*

- Use smaller, more familiar words, for example, *letter* instead of *correspondence, use* instead of *utilize, pay* for *recompense, also* for *furthermore.*

It's a challenge to write a letter that sends bad news but makes the customer come back with a smile. If you have to recall defective merchandise, refuse credit, or otherwise deny a request or refuse service, be firm but friendly, sympathetic, and reasonable. You may want to take refuge in more formal language that establishes an impersonal tone. This tone is not as appropriate when you need to placate a customer, but you can use it effectively to state firm decisions that cannot be appealed with further complaints. To do so, try the following:

- Use *the company* or *we* rather than *I.*

- Use passive voice rarely but wisely; for example, "the loan request could not be granted" removes an individual from the bad guy role because the person denying the request is hidden. Passive voice can also help avoid making accusations; for example, "When the seal on the computer housing was opened by someone other than an authorized repair center, the warranty was nullified" sounds better than "Because you broke the housing seal, you voided the warranty."

- Use courteous, respectful language that is clear and concise.

- Don't use big words to sound important.

- Use complete words rather than contractions.

In some cases, you might be able to add a positive element, offering an alternative or some means of recompense that might alleviate some of the customer's dissatisfaction. Be wary, though, of using some of the standard closing statements that tell customers you're delighted to serve them or that ask them to call if they need further assistance. If you've just turned down their request, they won't feel well served, and you don't want to leave room for misinterpreting your decision as less than final.

Routine replies—those that send neither good news nor bad—are brief and to the point, with little room for friendliness or formality. All letters to customers, however, can include some suggestion of the company's appreciation. Here are some examples:

- "Thank you for your continued interest in James Brothers."

- "We appreciate the opportunity to serve you."

- "If I can be of further assistance, please call my direct phone number, 555-2381."

- "Remember, we are always here to help you, 24 hours a day. We look forward to hearing from you soon."

Step 5: Write the First Draft

Armed with objectives, all relevant data, and an outline or list of points to cover, you are ready to begin your first draft. At this stage your only concern should be getting your thoughts down, either on paper or on disk. Don't worry about spelling, punctuation, or other mechanics. Polishing and refining will come later. Coherence isn't even important. It is quite acceptable to write sections out of sequence. If one part is easier to approach than another, then do it first. It is not unusual for the body of a document to be written before the beginning or the end. Knowing what to say in the middle is often easier than knowing how to start or close.

Remember that you don't have to share anything you write now. It doesn't have to be perfect. You are free to make additions, deletions, move paragraphs, etc. Knowing you will have the opportunity to revise your work should keep your anxiety to a minimum. If you are faced with something that is especially difficult to express, tackle something else and return to the complicated material later. Simply keep the words flowing.

One way to keep the words coming is to pretend you are actually talking to your reader. What would you say if he or she were seated across the table from you? How would you make sure your message is understood? Counter objections? Handle a negative response? Writing from this vantage point should help you achieve clarity and conciseness in your correspondence. Your letters and memos should also sound more natural. When you write as if you are speaking, you will be more aware of language that sounds overly formal, stilted, or ambiguous and can keep it out of your documents. But this doesn't mean the language should be too informal. Slang or obscenities, for example, would be quite inappropriate. Standard English should give you more than enough ways to express yourself powerfully, persuasively, and colorfully.

Following are a few ideas to help you develop your rough drafts:

- Try to write quickly. You are more likely to get out everything you need to say if you don't worry too much about how to say it. Now isn't the time for painstaking detail or long searches for the ideal words and phrases.

- Use simple language that says what you mean. Express ideas clearly and succinctly. In general, keep sentences and paragraphs short. Avoid overly long and complex sentences.

- Choose words that are familiar and descriptive. Precise words create a more accurate picture in the reader's mind than words that are vague. For example, saying that a minivan comfortably seats eight creates a stronger visual image than describing the minivan as roomy.

- Avoid clichés. These trite expressions will rob your writing of its personality and power.

- Complete your first draft before going back to revise and edit it. There is an old writing expression: "Don't get it right, get it written." Sound advice. Once you have something to work with, you can tinker with it as much as you like. But you can't fix what you haven't done.

- Once finished, set the first draft aside at least for a few hours. It will be easier to catch mistakes, missing information, inconsistencies, and other necessary corrections if you wrap up your work then return to it later with a fresh eye.

Step 6: Revise Your Work

With the first draft finished you are now ready for the final phase of the writing process: revising your work. This stage gives you one last chance to perfect your material.

Most revisions include three activities: revising, editing, and proofreading. This is where details definitely count.

Revising. Take a critical look at your first draft. Does its content reflect the objectives you developed at the project's outset? Have you presented everything on your outline or list of key points and covered it in sufficient depth? Is your message clear? Have you written from your reader's point of view? Is the material well organized? Have you verified the accuracy of your facts and included all relevant supporting data? Is the physical layout of your letter easy to follow?

Once you've identified weaknesses, you can usually correct them through rewrite and reorganization. If the letter doesn't flow well, you can strengthen the transitions so there is a more logical progression from one idea to the next. Missing information can be added; sections that are well written but poorly placed can be moved where they will fit better. Awkward phrases may either be deleted or reworked.

If your letter is particularly sensitive, consider asking someone else to review it. He or she may tell you how well you make your points, whether your arguments and explanations are unconvincing, and if certain passages are rambling or confusing. Use this feedback to polish your final piece.

Editing. When the draft has been revamped to your satisfaction, check spelling, punctuation, and grammar. Eliminate redundancies and make sure you have made the proper word choices. For these tasks a good dictionary and thesaurus are indispensable tools. If you are working on a computer that has spelling- and grammar-checking functions, use them. However, remember that the computer isn't infallible. You should still edit the material manually.

Proofreading. Before you send a letter to that important client, proofread it! This is truly the final opportunity to catch typos or other mistakes. Again, a spell checker is helpful, but it can't pick up the fact you typed *and* when you really meant *an* or *manger* for *manager*. It won't point out omissions, and it won't catch errors in your salutation—and the quickest way to ruin a good impression is to address your reader incorrectly. This is especially important when you are using computer mail-merge features to create many personalized letters. How do you think the reader who served as chair of an association reacted when she received a letter that began "Dear Ms. Chair . . . ?" Or the recipient of a letter which cozily advised "This is the perfect time, **INSERT ⋆ATIT⋆ ASUR**, to take advantage . . . ?"

Sending out a document with spelling and grammatical errors is not only embarrassing, it can lessen your credibility with your reader. It can convey the mistaken impression that you are careless or not very good with details. After taking the time to develop and revise a document, it's foolish not to take the last step to make sure it's right. Don't trust technology. Check your letters before they go out!

One final bit of advice is to give yourself enough time to write and revise your correspondence. Putting something off until the last minute only increases the prospect of failure. Of course tight deadlines are sometimes unavoidable. In those instances you may have to compromise and settle for good enough.

This six-step strategy provides an excellent framework for producing effective communications. Apply it consistently and you will complete your writing assignments more efficiently. More important, you will create clear, well-written correspondence that gets the desired results. One day you may even find yourself looking forward to the opportunity to put your thoughts on paper. When your colleagues begin to describe you as one of those natural born writers, smile and accept the compliment. No one has to know your ability to organize and present material is the result of a good formula and practice—and not just the touch of the Muses.

Should You Write or Call?

A letter is not always the best medium to use when communicating with customers, employees, suppliers, or competitors. Often a telephone call or a face-to-face meeting is more appropriate. For example, a customer who complains that a computer from your company freezes up when running a word-processing program needs a personal visit or a phone call, not a letter. A technical support staff member can talk the customer through the steps to resolve the problem over the telephone rather than risk misunderstanding by explaining the procedure in writing.

There is certainly no reason to invest the energy in writing a letter if another option is more time- and cost-effective. But bear in mind that there are times when you should put it in writing:

- Write a letter when you need a paper trail to document the history of a project, chronicle why one course of action was chosen over another, or track the progress of a negotiation and show what was agreed to and what remained unresolved. In certain human resources matters, documentation is essential, especially if litigation is a possibility.

- Write a letter when information needs to be relayed to a large number of individuals and there is no way to bring them together. You would never make phone calls to tell 25,000 customers you are raising prices!

When you are responding to a customer, choose the same medium, unless the customer specifically requests otherwise. The medium your customer chooses sends you an unwritten message about what your customer wants from you.

Letter, E-Mail, or Fax?

Should you send your letter through the mail, via fax, or via e-mail? Consider the following guidelines:

- Use a letter instead of a fax or e-mail if your letter describes a lengthy and complex problem.

- Use a fax when a prompt response is required.

- Use e-mail or fax when you need to broadcast information quickly to a large group.

- Use e-mail for overseas correspondence that must be handled quickly. Not only will your message get there quickly, it will also get there for a fraction of the cost of overseas postage or a long-distance telephone or fax call.

- Avoid e-mail when confidentiality is important. Anyone with know-how can access and read your messages or intercept them as they travel the Information Superhighway to their destination. This is important if you are in an industry that requires an extra level of security that may or may not exist on the Internet.

STYLE GUIDELINES FOR E-MAIL

- Keep e-mail short and direct.

- Because e-mail is like a memorandum, the salutation and closing or signature lines are not necessary but can be used to create a more personal communication.

- Use short one- or two-sentence paragraphs, and double-space between paragraphs. This makes the messages easier to read on the computer screen.

- Don't shout. How does one shout electronically? BY TYPING IN ALL CAPITAL LETTERS!!! AND BY USING TOO MANY EXCLAMATION POINTS!!

- Put an *asterisk* before and after any word you would ordinarily underline or italicize for emphasis. Internet communications, thus far, are strictly ASCII text, which means that accents or type variations such as bold or italic do not transfer.

- Acknowledge any e-mail message, either with a timely reply or with a quick note saying that the message was received, action will be taken, and a more specific reply will follow. Most e-mail software incorporates a reply feature—simply click on a reply button and a new message is automatically addressed to the individual who sent the original message.

Checklist for Effective Prose

☐ Open your letter with a hook that catches the reader's attention and provides a compelling reason to read the entire document.

☐ In the body of the document tell readers only what they need to know. Don't bog them down in unnecessary detail or repeat information they already know. Make your points, and if appropriate, show how your readers will benefit. Don't repeat yourself. Repetition is essential for speech, but on the printed page is unnecessary and counterproductive.

☐ Keep it short and simple. Use short sentences, short paragraphs, short letters. Be brief. The briefer you are, the more you are in command of the situation and the more likely you are to be read. By contrast, if you try to include too much information, some of it is sure to get lost. Stick to a single page, especially if you are writing a sales letter to a prospect or new customer. If you can't say everything on one page, use enclosures for additional information such as schedules or lists.

☐ Summarize longer letters. If you absolutely *must* write a letter longer than a page and a half, summarize the contents in the first paragraph if it's appropriate. A letter containing three choices of itinerary might be summarized like this:

THREE ITINERARIES:

We have prepared three different itineraries for you to choose from:

- via San Francisco, Honolulu, Fiji, Melbourne, Perth, Bangkok, New Delhi, Cairo, Paris, New York

- via Anchorage, Tokyo, Seoul, Omsk, Moscow, Oslo, Reykjavík, New York

- via San Juan, Rio de Janeiro, Capetown, Calcutta, Singapore, Christ Church, Santiago, Lima, Bogota, New York

Here are the details . . .

☐ Introduce and summarize with topic sentences. A sentence that expresses the main idea or thought in a paragraph is called a topic sentence. Use these key sentences to introduce or summarize the most important information or facts in your material.

❑ Use lists, bullet points, and if appropriate, headings to grab the eye, organize information, and break up long copy. Numbers can help, too—if they are used appropriately. Number items in a list only if they represent:

- a sequence—do this first, then this, then that

- a checklist—bring these five things to the contract signing; I need to know the following three things

- different parts of a whole—your car needs five kinds of service; here are the four most important features

❑ Use action verbs. A direct verb transfers action from one thing to another; for example, "man bites dog." An indirect verb is more static; in this case, "the dog is bitten by the man." Direct, active verbs make a stronger impact than indirect, inactive ones. Compare "applications should be submitted by May 30" to "submit the enclosed application by May 30"; "All these details should be discussed at your earliest convenience" to "We need to discuss these details. Would Thursday or Friday be better for you?" In each of these cases, straight talk is clearer and more forceful—and creates no doubt about what the reader is being asked to decide or do.

❑ Abandon hope! The word *hope* is so overused that it sounds weak, tentative, and unsure. It also focuses on the writer instead of the reader. Turn your emphasis around and abandon hope. Instead of tentatively saying "we hope the enclosed materials will meet your needs," try "you'll find the solution marked on the enclosed fact sheet." Instead of limply saying "We hope you will call us with any questions you may have," use the stronger "Questions? Call Marie Downs or me."

❑ Prune jargon—unless you are writing to members of a specific group, all of whom understand the shorthand terminology of their own sphere. In all other cases, replace jargon with clear phrases that anyone can recognize.

❑ Close your correspondence by summarizing the document's purpose or main points. Conclude by clearly stating what you want the reader to do.

❑ Consider adding a postscript to draw the reader's eye back over the letter. A postscript can be the most powerful part of a letter if it is used wisely. Don't just repeat something from the body of the letter.

STREAMLINE YOUR VOCABULARY

Letter writing sometimes does strange things to otherwise down-to-earth, friendly people. It can make us sound stuffy, staid, even pompous and stiff. We think that only by using big words can we project the image of the confident, knowledgeable professional. Wrong. The craft of letter writing has, over the years, developed deadwood that deserves to be chopped. Whenever you write a long and formal phrase, ask yourself whether you can shorten it. Don't use three words when one will do! The following list will help you think of short, snappy substitutes.

Stuffy and pompous	Better
due to the fact that	because
on account of	because
the reason is because	because
in spite of the fact that	despite, although
at the present time	now
in the near future	soon
reached a mutual agreement	agreed
at a rapid rate	rapidly
aware of the fact that	know
call attention to the fact that	notify, remind
conduct an investigation, test	investigate, test
engage in the alteration of	alter
in close proximity to	near
as of now, at the present time	now
at this point in time	now, today
in the near future	soon
in the recent past	recently
during the course of, during the time that	during, while
until such time as	until
with the possible exception of	except
in regard, with regard to	about
on condition that	provided
in the majority of situations	usually
at a high level of effectiveness	highly effective
for the purpose of, in order to	to
on the part of	by
in the area of	in
in the event that	if
the question as to whether	whether
there is no doubt but that	doubtless, no doubt
in a transparent manner	clearly, transparently

Part I

Letters to Customers

Because customers are at the heart of your business, letters to customers make up the bulk of all business correspondence. After all, there's plenty to say. Letters to customers can persuade, inform, compliment, contradict, apologize, and explain. They deliver bad news and good.

But no matter how bad the news you must deliver, it is *always* better to respond to customer concerns than to ignore them. That's because one of the most powerful motives behind the choices consumers make is how well they're treated. Research consistently shows that customers value service over other criteria, including price. They want to know they are *valued* by your company.

Those consumers—*your* customers—are your *business*, your reason for being. Without them, you'd cease to exist. Many a company has fallen for failing to provide the service that customers have come to expect. Although companies can exist for a while on one-time customers, word soon spreads that those who've tried your products or services aren't willing to return.

A well-written letter conveys your commitment to—and concern for—your customers. It also sells, for in essence *every* letter to a customer is a sales letter. You sell every time you respond quickly to inquiries and to your prospects' and customers' problems and concerns. You sell when you can turn customers down and give them a boost at the same time. You sell when you recognize people's accomplishments with congratulations, their contributions with thanks, their setbacks and losses with sympathy. Some of this you'll do in person or on the phone, of course, but when you put it in writing, your letter is a tangible reminder of your interest or concern.

Whether you need to introduce yourself and your product, reply to a query, solve a customer problem, or congratulate a customer, you will find an appropriate letter in the following pages. Study and use these letters, and your business—like your customer base—will grow.

Chapter 1

Prospecting for New Customers

The quest for new customers takes many forms, but it almost always includes a letter. This chapter includes a dozen different ways to structure letters to prospects, almost all of them short. That's because few people will read a letter that takes them more than a minute if they don't know the sender. Keep your prospecting letters to one page, unless you are sure of your reader's interest. If you absolutely must offer a lot of information, start by grabbing attention with a very short letter, then put supports, technical information, background, schedules, or prices in an enclosure. Always list any enclosures at the end of your letters. Not only will the list guide the person assembling the letter, it will provide a future record of what was sent and help steer readers past page one.

Stand-Alone Versus Open-the-Door Letters

Some products and services can sell themselves through a letter. The letter is the only connection with the customer before the reader responds by telephoning an order or mailing a check or turning up at a place or event. Sample letters 1.1, 1.2, 1.3, 1.9, 1.10, and 1.13 are good examples of stand-alone letters.

For other products and services, the letter is only the beginning. Its purpose is to arrange an interview or a demonstration or to urge the reader to request more in-depth information. Such open-the-door letters usually start the sales process for high-priced items, once-in-a-lifetime purchases, and customized products and services. Letters 1.4, 1.5, 1.6, 1.7, 1.8, 1.11, 1.12, 1.14, 1.15, 1.16, 1.17, 1.18, and 1.19 are open-the-door letters that can be adapted to more complex selling situations.

Features, Benefits, and Motivations

Are you selling haircuts or self-esteem? Values or comfort? Germ-killing detergent or peace of mind? More copies per minute or more time for creative work and relaxation? The one thing you're probably *not* selling is your product or service. You're selling what it can do for the buyer.

Every product or service sells because of three things:

1. features—what the product or service is

2. benefits—what the product or service does

3. motivations—what's in it for the customer; how your product or service makes life better

A simplification might be: *has, does, means.* A product *has* features, *does* something that is a benefit, and *means* something that is a motivation. For example, an employee relocation service:

- *has* affiliations with 2,700 realtors, 20 moving companies, and 400 personal relocation counselors in 46 states and 20 foreign countries, plus reduced-price travel arrangements, computerized school searches, substantial discounts on furnishings for the new home, etc. (*Features*)

- *does* provide fast, complete, one-stop relocation services for your employees and their families at a lower overall cost than if you contracted individually with the various services; it probably decreases employee stress and increases satisfaction, morale, and family support, thus providing greater productivity. (*Benefits*)

- *means* you as an employer have greater flexibility in reassigning personnel, leading to a sense of power, control, and prestige. (*Motivations*)

Or a new electronic door lock:

- *has* a sophisticated sound-analyzing computer chip

- *does* recognize and respond to authorized voices

- *means* extra security against intruders, plus you'll never be locked out again if you forget or lose your key

Your job is to demonstrate that the *features* provide *benefits* that create powerful *motivations* to buy. Make the connection unmistakable. Prove what you're selling is worth far more in satisfaction than it will cost. Some benefits, as in the following, must be spelled out:

> **Better Density.** *Our cartridges measured a density of 1.4 compared to 1.29 for Standard's cartridge, using a densitometer. (A higher number means a darker image.)*

But never assume that cost, functions, or speed will automatically transform into *cheaper, more convenient,* or *faster.* Don't even assume that *cheaper, more convenient,* or *faster* will be perceived as real benefits by a customer who may be more concerned about reliability, control, or status. You are responsible for creating the chain of associations. For example:

> *More copies per second means your staff will spend less time in the back room doing paperwork. They can be out on the floor where they belong, serving customers and making sales.*

An easy way to tie the characteristics of what you're selling to your prospects' wants and needs is sales trainer, speaker, and consultant Bill Bethel's "So-Because Rule." If you start by writing about a feature, continue with "so . . . ," then show how that feature produces a benefit. If you start with the benefit, follow with "because . . . ," and specify the feature. It doesn't matter which way you do it:

> *We've eliminated 90 percent of the paperwork so you can process your claim in less than five minutes.*

Or:

> *You can process your claim in less than five minutes because we've eliminated 90 percent of the paperwork.*

These benefits may or may not be motivations in themselves. If the motivation for experiencing a specific benefit won't be overwhelmingly obvious in the mind of the reader, spell it out. Put your hunches and solid research about your prospects' motivations to work when you craft your sales letter. If you are writing to lawyers who want to be seen as competent and in control but have neglected to purchase insurance, you might start by acknowledging the reader's importance, and then offer a guilt-free, labor-free way to apply for a group-term plan. Likewise, a letter to environmentally conscious computer owners might sell recycled printer cartridges by highlighting environmental benefits as well as performance and durability. Find out your prospects' motivational buttons, and push them.

When you can answer the question "What's in it for me?" vividly and truthfully, you've probably made the sale!

Follow-Through Checklist

When a letter doesn't get the response you want, go back and figure out why.

❑ Did your letter(s) go to the right person? Are you sure this person has the power to buy? The interest?

❑ Did you grab the reader in the first sentence or two while making it clear why you were writing?

❑ Should you try emphasizing a different benefit or motivation? Did you address the most important features and benefits from your potential customer's point of view?

❑ Did you confront and overcome potential objections?

❑ Was your letter easy to read?

❑ Was the tone of your letter appropriate for your product or service and your readers?

❑ Was your letter too long? Too short?

Keep track of what works and what doesn't. It isn't always possible to know exactly why a particular letter doesn't get a strong response, but if you analyze the success of each communication, a pattern will emerge eventually.

> Remember: a great sales letter should be like fast food. Be sure your reader can get through it quickly and pleasurably.

1.1   *Spark Reader's Thinking with a Checklist*

Strong opening promises an easy solution.

This short sentence tells *what* the company does and for *whom* its products are appropriate.

Checklist helps reader think of a variety of applications for these gifts.

Underlined phrases stress key benefits.

Dear Ms. Gomez:

Just one phone call, and we'll solve MOST of your gift-giving problems.

We create ready-to-go and customized gift baskets for your clients, suppliers, coworkers, friends, and family. Choose from our catalogue, or consult with one of our expert stylists to design your own basket.

Our June selections include:

- ❑ congratulation
- ❑ thanks for your help
- ❑ special World Series baskets
- ❑ Father's Day
- ❑ graduation
- ❑ birthday
- ❑ anniversary
- ❑ shower gifts
- ❑ new baby
- ❑ retirement
- ❑ get well

We'll provide

- any quantity. Order one basket or 10,000.

- plain or lavish. We'll make your basket as simple or as elaborate as you wish.

- rush delivery. Two-hour delivery is available for most items.

Call us at (333) 000-0000 and let us help make all your special times even more special.

Sincerely,

1.2 *Paint a Vivid Picture*

Creative-writing skills paint an unforgettable picture of the reader interacting with the product, starting with the key sentence, "Visualize this."

Boldface type highlights product name throughout.

Free trial offer encourages readers to respond quickly.

Dear Mr. Fabiano:

Visualize this: You're approaching your house on a dark night. Suddenly, all the lights go on and a scanner tells you if anyone is in your house or yard.

I'm talking about a new device called **SafeHouse** that lets you come home to comfort and safety with just the press of a button. And you can reverse the process when you leave, turning off the lights once you have locked the door, descended the steps, and left the yard. Amazingly, **SafeHouse** weighs just four ounces and fits in pocket or purse.

If you send me the enclosed reply card by June 2, you can try **SafeHouse** free for 30 days. You have nothing to risk. Nothing to lose. And maybe a lot to gain.

Sincerely,

ENCL: reply card

1.3   *Pose and Answer Questions*

Opening stresses need for the product.

Dear Ms. Gannett:

With the recent outbreaks of dangerous Lyme disease, your need for tick protection for yourself and your family has never been so critical. Now there is a proven, successful way to rid your yard and grounds of ticks for three months. It's the **Allied Tick-Kicker** and it's guaranteed!

Question-and-answer format conveys important information in a way that engages the reader. Asking "why is this product different?" allows immediate presentation of key benefits.

Why is the Tick-Kicker different?

- No poisons endanger your children and pets. **Tick-Kicker** attracts ticks with special low-frequency sounds and kills them with microwaves.

- Nothing disrupts native ecology. Only ticks are affected.

This letter could also ask "Who needs XYZ?" (with a story about someone who suffered by not using the product), and "How much can you save?" (with charts and figures).

Who already uses the Tick-Kicker?

The city and county of Middleville, the East State Park Authority, and the Association of Day Camps have all mandated the use of **Tick-Kicker** for the past three years.

What proof do you have that it works?

Three independent studies have shown that **Tick-Kicker** is 100 percent effective in eliminating ticks for a minimum of three months. (We'll provide full test data on request.)

Letter asks only three or four questions so it is short and easy to read. Boldface type highlights each question.

How can you learn more?

Just return the enclosed postcard or call me at (800) 000-0000.

Sincerely,

ENCL: postcard

1.4   *Stress Benefits*

This letter focuses on benefits by downplaying what the product is—short-term furnished apartments—and stressing what it does.

Using actual figures reminds the reader of how much money is at stake.

This paragraph and the next are packed with concrete benefits of apartment living.

Repeating and highlighting the main benefit—saving money—brings the letter to a strong close.

Listing enclosures grabs attention and steers readers past page one.

Dear Ms. Ishima:

If your firm has new hires, interns, or business associates coming to the Denver area, we can save you *half the cost* of the average hotel room!

The March 1999 issue of *Business Travel* (copy enclosed) says that the average daily cost of accommodations is $148.23, plus $68.49 for food—an average total cost of $216.72 per person per day.

We offer short-term, fully furnished, spacious apartments throughout the metropolitan area as an affordable, convenient, and homelike alternative for people on the move. Corporate billing is acceptable.

Our apartments provide twice the space and comfort of an average hotel room and feature fully equipped kitchens with cooking and dining utensils, linens (for bath and bed), televisions with cable service, local phone service, and telephone answering machines. Weekly maid service is included at select properties.

In addition, guests can enjoy a range of sports and recreational facilities—among them swimming pools, spas, tennis courts, and fitness centers—AT NO EXTRA COST.

While rates vary according to size of apartment, length of stay, and extra services provided, the cost is generally less than half the cost of the average hotel room!

Give us a call today at (800) 000-0000 or send us a fax at (000) 000-0000 for further information or for reservations.

Sincerely,

ENCL: *Business Travel* article, "Your Home in Denver"

1.5   *Stress Benefits* and *Motivations*

The benefits this company offers are linked with a strong motivation— hating to clean house.

Subhead stresses a primary benefit and breaks up a boring page.

This subhead zeroes in on a motivation and introduces two benefits that eliminate potential sources of guilt.

Letter stresses that the prospect can enjoy a clean house without worrying about toxic products or unfair wages and labor practices.

Dear Mrs. Lenovich:

We hate cleaning as much as you do. That's why we started Allied Comprehensive Cleaning Services, an exceptional service for fastidious people. ACCS has a *spotless* three-year record of providing superior housekeeping services to the most discriminating families.

<u>No Hassles!</u>

Never again will you have to scrub, vacuum, dust, clean, polish, disinfect, deodorize, launder, sort, mend, or wax!

No complicated record keeping. You'll have no payroll-deduction or unemployment-insurance forms to file because we handle it all.

No interviewing, hiring, checking references, finding replacements. Just one phone call guarantees that our skilled professionals arrive whenever you want them, on a regular schedule or as needed.

No fear of loss. All our professionals are fully bonded and insured against damage or loss of any kind.

<u>No Guilt!</u>

All cleaning products are nontoxic and absolutely environmentally safe. We use no harmful cleaners or solvents.

All our employees are well-paid professionals who receive full medical and dental benefits, plus two weeks paid vacation each year. Their high level of satisfaction is reflected in their exceptional service, dedication, and helpful attitude.

Enclosed is a brochure explaining our service in more detail. May we have the pleasure of offering you further information?

Sincerely,

ENCL: *Clean Forever: Your Answer to Dirt and Disorder*

1.6   *Address a Problem*

Letter starts by alerting reader to the problem, then explains how the company can quickly solve the problem.

This paragraph elaborates on the problem in order to better sell the company's ability to solve it.

Another approach: alert the reader to the problem, and then offer easy-to-spot alternatives that let the reader quickly grasp the gist of the letter.

Dear Mr. Limanowski:

Just when you thought you had your payroll system set up to run smoothly through the end of the year, the government has changed the regulations. **PayMaster**, with more than twenty years as the state's leading payroll consultant, is ready to advise medium and small businesses on how to negotiate this new mine field of payroll reporting and deductions.

Why not let our **PayMaster** professionals show you how to comply with the new laws on:

- health-coverage reporting, an enormous undertaking that can be reduced to manageability with prudent planning

- voluntary and involuntary deduction requirements, a leading contender for payroll disaster

- The accelerated deposit rule, which may give your company only one day to figure and deposit payroll taxes

Perhaps your people have the time and expertise to research and implement these regulatory changes so that you'll avoid expensive losses and penalties. If not, we stand ready to serve you.

Sincerely,

1.7 *Address a Problem*

This short letter gets straight to the point: for solutions to floor and shelving space problems, call Allied, already used by many prestigious colleagues.

Dear Ms. Long:

Is floor space a problem in your library? Do you need more shelving capacity or more study space?

We can create it for you. Allied Shelf Systems are already used by some of the most prestigious libraries and corporations in the world.

May we show you how Allied Shelf Systems could work for you, at no cost or obligation? Our toll-free number is (800) 000-0000.

Sincerely,

ENCL: *High Density Mobile Storage*

The brochure continues the problem–solution approach by showing how other libraries and corporations have used Allied products to solve space problems.

1.8 *Overcome Objections*

Because this letter is persuasive and well-organized, it can get away with requiring more than one page.

Dear Mr. Schuster:

Your $1,000 rent check can cover a $158,000+ home loan. Today's incredible buyers' market is *your* best chance to buy a home. With interest rates so affordably low, your monthly mortgage will probably be less than you now pay for rent.

Your rent payment of	Covers a loan of*
$600/month	$94,900
$800/month	$126,550
$1,000/month	$158,200
$1,200/month	$189,850

* BASED ON A.P.R. OF 6.795%

Don't let lack of information stand between you and your first home. Why wait when you can afford more now?

(continued)

Quotes quickly pull the reader through various objections and the company's solutions. To use this approach in your letters, imagine all the reasons your readers might reject you, and address those issues head-on.

Underline or boldface objections to catch the reader's eye.

"I don't have enough for a down payment."

Conventional financing is now available to qualified buyers with as little as 5 percent down—and 2 percent of that amount can be from gifts. FHA loans are available with 3 percent down, and VA loans with nothing down.

"I'm waiting until I can afford something nicer."

With interest rates at record lows, you can probably qualify for that nicer home now. Keep in mind that if interest rates go up just a few percentage points, you will pay hundreds of dollars more each month to borrow the same amount of money. Qualifying for a higher monthly payment will also require a larger income.

"I'm waiting to see if prices go down more."

Home prices have been stable for some time now. As the market continues to recover, you can expect higher prices and less affordable interest rates. By buying now, the cycle of recovery will work in your favor, as the home you own appreciates in value.

"Finding out how much I can afford takes a lot of time and paperwork."

You can be prequalified within minutes in any of our offices. A mortgage representative will use a laptop computer to show you what mortgage amount you qualify for, based on your answers to a few simple questions. As a prequalified buyer, you can shop for a home with confidence.

Tell us what you now pay for monthly rent. You'll get back a printout showing how much that payment can buy you today, plus some sample listings in that price range. Just call us at (800) 000-0000 or stop by any of our offices.

Sincerely,

1.9 *Issue an Invitation*

Key information about what-when-where is presented in the opening paragraph, making it impossible to miss on first reading and easy to retrieve later.

Each bullet describes a benefit or feature.

Stressing the support or sponsorship of the reader's office or industry gives more reason for the reader to accept the invitation.

Postscript adds a brief personal appeal to reader.

Dear Jack,

If you feel like it's time for you to take a break and get a fresh look at the latest in the world of Esperanto, you may want to join us at:

The 15th Annual

ESPERANTO TRANSLATORS' GETAWAY

Friday/Saturday October 18–19

Riverview Ranch

Here are just some of the highlights:

- Share the world premiere of the brand new breakthrough *International Esperanto Dictionary* on CD-ROM.

- Hear speakers from 11 nations who will update you on the latest advances and developments.

- Meet Dr. David Joranson, who will be discussing new careers in Esperanto. Several personnel representatives of international corporations will also be present.

- Swim, ride, play tennis, or just loaf. Full spa facilities are available.

We've had a lot of support from the Northern State Esperanto Association in getting this important event off the ground. With their help and input, we're sure this weekend is going to be a rewarding experience for everyone involved.

Sincerely,

ENCL: schedule and reservation forms

P.S. Bob Harron says "Hi," and that he hopes to see you there.

1.10   *Issue an Invitation*

Key information is stressed in the first paragraph. Since readers are already going to the convention, the booth number is more important than dates or location.

Personal demonstrations of a respected product and a new one give readers two reasons to stop by the booth.

Postscript adds one more reason to visit: a free gift.

Dear Ms. Forbes:

When you attend the Dingbat Association Conference in San Francisco next week, Acme Doodads invites you to stop at Booth 22 at the Moscone Center.

We're excited about what our innovative new line of Doodads could do for your company, and we welcome the chance to show you in person.

Rod LaRoque and I will be there to demonstrate hot new applications of our classic Gizmo, and to introduce our Thingamajig, which has gotten raves in all the trade papers.

Looking forward to seeing you in San Francisco!

Sincerely,

P.S. Bring the enclosed card and we'll swap it for a free mini-Gizmo.

1.11   *Take the Two-Step Approach*

Because this conference means a considerable financial commitment, this letter's two-step approach softens up a resistant reader first with an overview, and promises details a few days later.

The first letter presents the big idea.

Dear Mr. Gengler:

A unique and historic trade conference will take place this December in the People's Republic of China. I would like to extend a formal invitation to you and another member of your firm to be delegates to the Pacific Rim Trade Conference. It is sponsored by Trade Programs International under the aegis of the U.S. State Department.

The delegation will consist of approximately 200 representatives from our industry. It will depart Los Angeles on Saturday, December 7th, and return on Monday, December 16th.

In a few days you will receive more details from Mr. Allan Jones, vice president of our trade association. In the meantime, if you need any preliminary information, please call me.

Sincerely,

Stanley Smith
PRESIDENT

The follow-up asks for a decision.

Dear Mr. Gengler:

A few days ago you received a letter from Mr. Stanley Smith regarding your firm's participation in the Pacific Rim Trade Conference in the People's Republic of China this December. The purpose of my letter is to provide additional information about the project and the procedures involved in joining the delegation.

[Include lots of additional information and supports here.]

Both Mr. Smith and I hope that you can become a member of this project. We look forward to hearing from you.

Sincerely,

Allan Jones
VICE PRESIDENT

1.12   *Take the Two-Step Approach*

Three kinds of business letters are almost sure to be opened: those from the IRS, a lawyer, and a famous person. Here's a real letter from someone who will probably catch the reader's attention.

A second letter from Speaker Foley will spell out exactly what support is requested.

BILL CLINTON

Dear John,

Once again, I need your help.

In 1992, you and I fought for the Presidency on a platform based on new hope for this country.

And since my inauguration over one year ago, we have seen the spark of that historic election reignite the flame of hope in America, and its intensity grows each day.

But unfortunately, there are many who want to extinguish that flame simply to further their own political ambitions.

They only want to see this Administration fail—with little, or no, regard for the effects on our fellow citizens. Their actions threaten to slow, if not stop, the initiatives that you and I set in motion in November of 1992.

During the 1992 campaign, as a major leader within our Party, you played a significant role in my election as President of the United States.

Now I must ask you to take the second step in our journey toward progress. I have asked Speaker Foley to contact you concerning a project that is key to the success of this Administration and our initiatives to change this nation.

I urge you to think about what the Speaker has to say, and I hope you'll step forward and help me.

John, ever since I accepted our Party's nomination for President, you've backed me up. And I know I can count on you now.

_____

(Signature)

1.13   *Stress Exclusivity*

When status or membership is a strong motivation, stressing the exclusivity of the event or offer will boost response.

Dear Ms. Wilson:

As a past client of Prestige-Plus Motors, you may be interested to know that our marketing firm has been retained to reduce the Prestige-Plus inventory of previously owned luxury vehicles.

More than $2.5 million in recent and classic models will be offered to the public, starting November 10, at our South City facility.

However, we are pleased to inform you that, as a current patron of Prestige-Plus, *you* may preview these vehicles on <u>Wednesday, November 7</u>. Simply bring this letter with you for admission between 9:00 a.m. and 6:00 p.m. All phone inquiries should be directed to Everett Petherbridge at (000) 000-0000.

Sincerely,

P.S. Naturally, your current relationship with Prestige-Plus entitles you to immediate delivery and on-the-spot credit.

The postscript addresses two additional benefits available only to current customers.

1.14   *Ask for a Meeting or Interview*

Dramatic tale catches interest among accountants who face similar quandaries.

Dear Ms. Campbell:

What's wrong with this true story?

A man inherited a thriving company from his father. An accountant, advised by an attorney, set up a trust to protect the client's assets from judgments resulting from any potential lawsuit. Not only did the client thus give up control of his hard-earned assets, he found to his dismay that the trust could be penetrated. He lost his home and business.

As an accountant, your relationship with clients is based on protecting their assets. In today's volatile business climate—with litigation at an all-time high—you need credible backup you can rely on for unbiased advice. We specialize in advising accountants. We work *with you* to judgment-proof your clients' property. You retain full control over your client relationship.

Our colleague, attorney Roland Young, has experience as a federal prosecutor in the tax division of the Department of Justice. He knows which strategies stand up legally . . . and which are easily penetrated.

Bold type highlights the main benefit provided by these legal consultants—solutions that withstand judgments.

His methods create an impassable legal obstacle in the path of potential judgments.

Ask for a meeting, interview, or telephone appointment whenever a product can't be sold effectively without personal contact. This attention-getting letter alerts readers to expect a telephone call—if they haven't been moved by the message to call the sender first!

Read the enclosed fact sheet and resume. I'll call you within several days to discuss the next step to bolster protection for your clients.

Sincerely,

ENCL: fact sheet and resume

(Used with permission of Ann Bloch)

1.15   *Ask for Phone Interview*

This letter, sent in advance of a phone call, gets the attention of hard-to-reach prospects.

The enclosure warms up the reader by explaining more about the product or service.

Dear Mr. Smith:

Because of your heavy schedule, I am taking this means to introduce my company and myself.

The enclosed article from *Business News Monthly*, "Are Your Employees Costing You Money . . . Or Making You Money?" points out dramatically how easily payroll dollars can be wasted. Our firm is currently serving thousands of businesses with a simple and inexpensive supplement to management's efforts. Our clients tell us we have upgraded the performance of their people and reduced their payroll costs substantially.

Perhaps you would like to evaluate our idea in terms of profit for your organization. I will contact you within the next few days for an appointment.

Sincerely,

ENCL: "Are Your Employees Costing You Money . . . Or Making You Money?"

(Used with permission of Lee Boyen)

1.16   *Fax for Phone Interview*

A fax can get your prospect's attention if it is short and arresting. This one, sent to 100 target physicians, got a 19 percent response in just a few days.

To: Dr. Jonah Marshall

Because you are one of the best, your patients chose you.
Wouldn't you like to offer your patients new procedures?
With future health-care reimbursement in question, would patient pay procedures benefit your office?
Did you know that preceptorship training for the unique laser skin resurfacing and laser blepharoplasty is available?
Please call (800) 555-3646 and ask for Mr. René Chlumecky.

(Used with permission of René Chlumecky)

1.17   *Ask for a Reply*

Dear Ms. Masters:

You're a very busy woman!

I haven't been able to reach you on the phone, so I'm actually resorting to the post office.

If you would answer the questions below in the blank spaces and return this letter to me in the enclosed stamped envelope, we will both know whether there is a mutual advantage in talking on the phone.

1. Do you ever have a meeting where you hire an outside speaker?

   _____

2. My topics are: Communication Skills, Customer Service, and Sales. (Brochure enclosed.) Do those subjects fit any of your future plans?

   _____

3. If you use outside speakers on these subjects, what can I do to help you decide to hire me for your next meeting?

   _____

I believe my training and experience will make my message unique and valuable to your organization. I would like an opportunity to prove it to you.

Cordially,

ENCL: SASE and brochure

Always make answering easier than *not* answering. By enclosing a self-addressed, stamped envelope, the writer ensures a good response because most people can't stand to waste postage. They usually end up scribbling and mailing a reply because it's the easiest thing to do.

1.18   *Ask for a Reply*

Well-designed reply coupons can save prospecting and qualifying time.

> Thank you for your interest in a Coherent Laser. I enjoyed the opportunity to talk to you about our products and look forward to speaking with you again soon.
>
> So that I don't contact you before you're ready, please take a minute to fill out and return the reply card below.
>
> _____
> *(signature)*
>
> -
> *(fold on dotted line)*
>
> ### WHERE DO WE GO FROM HERE?
>
> ❏ Please call to set up an appointment.
> ❏ Please call. We have additional questions.
> ❏ We are still interested and awaiting approval.
> ❏ Our purchase is on hold.
>   Call back: _____
>
>   Contact: _____
>
> ❏ We've already purchased a laser.
> ❏ We are no longer interested in a laser.
>
> _____
> *(customer's name)*
>
> [cut & paste LOGO]

Checklist of possible responses helps potential customers clarify their needs and options and indicate whether a salesperson should call.

(Used with permission of Stephen P. Duddy)

1.19   *Contact Cooled-Off Hot Prospects*

Opening reminds reader of previous inquiry.

New materials give details about this year's schedule.

Closing is a "truthful stimulator"—a factual statement that also urges the reader to act quickly.

Dear Mr. Hansen:

In 1998, you asked for information about Sheila Murray Bethel to consider her as a potential speaker at one of your conferences or meetings.

Either Sheila was not chosen or her schedule did not make her available on the dates you requested. In either case, we did not have the pleasure of doing business with you in 1998.

Are you planning any meetings this year where you will be using an outside speaker? I have enclosed a new brochure about Sheila to remind you who she is and what she does. If you would like further information, including a video brochure, we will be happy to send it for your consideration.

Sheila's book *Making a Difference* has sold more than 80,000 copies and is now out in paperback as well. She has spoken for every type of organization, large and small, in every state plus seventeen foreign countries.

Her speaking schedule fills up quickly, so if you have any interest in Sheila as a potential speaker in the coming year, please let us hold a date for you pending your final decision. Thanks for your interest.

Cordially,

Chapter 2

Developing Prospects and Customers

O nce you've broken ground with a prospect, your letters can focus on closing the sale and developing business. While this chapter contains letters that respond to queries, welcome new customers, and help keep accounts active, it's important to note that not every letter needs to sell a product. In fact, when a long-term association between customer and supplier is desirable or essential to the selling process, many of your letters will sell your relationship: trust, esteem, rapport. Your letters will demonstrate that you and your company are indispensable to the smooth functioning of your customers' business or personal lives.

Such "tickler" letters can offer relevant news and tips:

I just heard your firm will be opening a new facility in Detroit next spring. This might be a good opportunity for us to . . .

How are the new regulations going to affect your Scranton plant? I've done some research for another client in your area, and I'd be glad to send you a copy . . .

Ticklers can be service pieces, offering market news or helpful information without any direct references to buying something. Some people even send regular newsletters. A note offering congratulations on a promotion or a grandchild or sincere thanks for a customer's order or assistance can also serve as a tickler. (Letters like these are covered in Chapter 7, "Expressing Thanks and Congratulations.")

When your letter's goal is to help build a relationship, take a moment to determine what you want your letter to do. Once your goals are clear, write them down and check your first draft to be sure you are addressing them. Then let your readers know exactly what response you'd like. If you are responding to a customer query, use the format in the box below to guide your prose.

FORMAT FOR A TYPICAL LETTER RESPONDING TO A CUSTOMER QUERY

1. Start by describing enclosures.

2. Offer a brief sales pitch.

3. Add a truthful stimulator, if appropriate—a special offer, a limited-time offer, or some other incentive for making a prompt purchase decision.

4. Close on a hopeful note.

2.1   *Answering a Query*

First sentence recaps the question; second sentence tells where to find the answer. (If catalogue is lengthy, mention page number where product is described.)

Providing names and numbers of contact firms is an excellent use of a third-party recommendation. It adds credibility, demonstrates good relationships with customers, and reassures reader the company can be trusted.

Additional technical information shows the company is interested in providing thorough, complete service.

Closing lets the prospect control the next step of the selling process.

Dear Mr. Hubbard:

You asked about our Dual Star triple-press extractor. Here is a copy of our latest catalogue with a full description.

Your offices happen to be near several other manufacturing firms that have installed this system. One especially, Pull-It, Inc., in Eastville, has used two Dual Star extractors for the past five years. You may want to talk to Francis Lederer about their experiences, both with improved quality control and cost-performance return. A list of contact names and phone numbers is enclosed.

I am also sending you our *Production Specifications Manual* because you may want a more detailed picture of how the dual valves will interact with your present system.

You can call me at (333) 000-0000 when you've had a chance to look over this material. I am eager to answer your questions and to prepare you a savings estimate based on your requirements.

Sincerely,

ENCL: 1999 catalogue
       Production Specifications Manual
       list of purchasers

2.2   *Saying Thanks for Sales Call*

This note thanks a busy prospect for her time and enthusiasm and reminds her that the next step in the sales process is underway.

Main benefit is stressed again so the prospect can present it to partners who will approve the purchase.

Because the salesperson didn't get to make a presentation to the other decision makers, the main selling points are reiterated in easy-to-read bullets so the reader can relay them, a good tactic for situations in which information needs to reach others.

Dear Gerda,

I would like to thank you again for your time today and your enthusiasm about putting the Allied Tracking Technology Program to work for XYZ. I am preparing a proposal and contract to your specifications, and they should be ready within a few days.

I know you have to get approval from your partners to institute this system at XYZ. If they express any reluctance to move forward with Allied, please stress that since the payback is so extraordinary, it's a move that makes good economic sense.

When you talk to Franco and Jill, you can emphasize that:

- A year from now at the very latest, according to your own calculations, you will have recovered your investment and will have a system that can serve you for many years to come.

- Three hundred local firms now use the Allied system.

- Allied has the financial strength and stability to maintain ongoing research and development. We were number 25 on the *Forbes* 1999 list of the top 200 small companies, based on financial analysis.

- Only Allied designs, manufactures, tests, markets, installs, and supports all of its products directly. We offer the state of the art in the industry.

We look forward to a productive partnership with XYZ. I'm eager to answer any further questions and to assist you in your selling efforts.

Sincerely,

2.3   *Saying Thanks for Sales Call*

After saying thanks, this letter becomes a sales letter, neatly tying Allied's benefits to XYZ's goals.

Boldface headings announce each feature and let reader locate key information. Text shows how the feature benefits XYZ.

Dear Roberto:

It was a genuine pleasure meeting you yesterday and getting to know the specific needs and issues that apply to XYZ's long-term requirements.

Some important ways that Allied can help XYZ reach those goals are:

Our full-service research department: We can respond to your short-term and long-term research needs more economically than you can in-house, while guaranteeing you full proprietary control over results.

Our full marketing and promotional services: Allied's promotional people, the tops in their field, are available to you on an as-needed basis, but you pay *only* for time plus materials, *not* the commission usually charged by outside organizations.

Our site-planning resources: Allied currently manages 12 million square feet of prime real estate in the area, and represents landlords of another 40 million square feet. As XYZ's needs change, you will have immediate access to a substantial number of existing and planned sites for your consideration.

Thank you for meeting with us. We look forward to putting Allied's resources to work for you and XYZ.

Sincerely,

2.4   *Saying Thanks for Contact at Convention*

Everyone who stops by a convention booth should be promptly thanked. Use this short form letter to acknowledge a visit and reply to specific comments or questions.

List benefits and features instead of burying them in long paragraphs—and keep the list short.

Dear Ms. Buher:

Thank you for visiting our booth at last month's state expo. The show was quite successful, with an overwhelming response to our new product introductions. [You can add comments about reader's interests or questions here.]

To recap Allied's newest products for you:

- [benefit A because of feature A]

- [benefit B because of feature B]

- [benefit C because of feature C]

- [benefit D because of feature D]

We appreciate your interest at the show and look forward to discussing these innovative ideas with you in the future.

Sincerely,

Postscript tells reader to expect a call with more information.

P.S. [Name] will call you soon about the [name of product that might interest prospect].

2.5   *Welcoming a New Customer*

A gracious welcome letter tells this new customer the company takes the relationship seriously and stands ready to serve.

Important material is highlighted in a separate paragraph.

Specific features are reviewed so the customer knows how to obtain important benefits, such as 24-hour ordering or discount cards.

Dear Ms. O'Neill:

It is my great pleasure to welcome you as a new Allied purchaser. We look forward to serving you for many years to come.

Your [documentation, booklet, first statement, membership card] is enclosed.

Some features that may be especially [useful, interesting, important] to you as a new customer are:

- [benefit, feature]

- [benefit, feature]

- [benefit, feature]

If I can ever be of assistance, please call me toll free at (800) 000-0000.

Cordially,

ENCL: [documentation, booklet, first statement, membership card]

2.6   *Welcoming a New Customer*

Opening is short and succinct.

Boldface headings highlight important contents and information.

Two important benefits help the sale "stick" by reassuring customer he or she has made the right decision.

Dear Ms. Nguyen:

Welcome to FAST-AIR, and thank you for requesting this Air Starter Kit.

Shipping kit enclosed: You'll find everything you need to start shipping and saving today. Your FAST-AIR account number is 0000000000. For your convenience, a card with your account number is also enclosed.

Be sure to notice two very important FAST-AIR guarantees:

1. **Refund guarantee**: However you send your shipment (FAST-AIR Next-Day Air, FAST-AIR 2nd-Day Air, or FAST-AIR 3-Day Select), if your shipment is not delivered by the time we promise, we'll refund the shipping charges.

2. **24-hour hot-line tracking**: Whenever you call our 24-hour tracking hot line to check on a shipment's tracking status, we'll have your answer in seconds. If we ever take longer than 30 minutes, we'll refund the shipping charges.

In choosing FAST-AIR, you've made an important decision for your business. Our on-time delivery record and money-back guarantees are second to none.

Sincerely,

ENCL: shipping kit, account card

2.7 *Cultivating with "Ticklers"*

"Ticklers" are any letters or notes that are sent to keep communication open and to remind people of your existence and interest. Use these simple examples to stimulate tickler letters of your own.

Dear John,

Haven't talked to you for some time and thought I'd just say, "Hello, can I be of service?"

Best wishes,

Dear Florence,

You immediately came to mind when I read about [the trade agreement, terrible floods, the Supreme Court decision, XYZ's exciting new patent]. How are you [doing, handling it, holding up, celebrating]?

Sincerely,

Dear Reno,

When I looked at the calendar this morning, I immediately thought of you.

A year ago this week, we were in the midst of [installing your new system, closing on your house, stamping out fires together at XYZ, reveling over your triumph, commiserating over your setback, trying to imagine the end of this project].

What a [difficult, exciting, rewarding, challenging] time! How are things going for you now?

Cordially,

2.8   *Keeping Customers Active*

Special offer entices customers to place a new order.

Bulleting and underlining draw attention to benefits.

Dear Ms. McBride:

Now *you* get to decide if the new products we've introduced during the past year were worth the enormous effort we made to meet the changing needs in your industry. To be sure you have a chance to find out for yourself, we're offering the following:

- A 20 percent discount: Just use the enclosed order form to try the newest technology while saving 20 percent.

- Billing: You don't have to send payment with your order to receive this discount, as long as you use this special order form.

Thanks again for all your support in the past. We'll continue to work hard to bring you the most advanced products, and we're always eager to hear your comments and suggestions.

Sincerely,

ENCL: order form

2.9   *Retaining Customers*

Short opening boldly states the problem.

Advantages and disadvantages presentation adds clarity and humor to this very well-written letter.

Members may already know the features, but the benefits need to be sold again to secure a renewal.

Dear Mr. Stone:

Your membership expires this month.
Advantages of renewing immediately:

- uninterrupted access to our two four-star downtown locations, just a few steps from your office, with complete gym and spa facilities, including our new lava-rock steam room and jai alai courts; open 6 a.m. to midnight weekdays

- renewed energy, weight maintenance, body tone, and vigor

- the exciting menu at Members Only, our vegetarian health bar that gives new meaning to "Power Lunch" (Will you ever forget Helga's award-winning coleslaw? And Helga's homemade carrot cake is irresistible.)

Disadvantages of renewing immediately: Helga's homemade carrot cake is irresistible.
Think about it.

Sincerely,

2.10 *Recapturing Former or Inactive Customers*

It's impossible to correct a problem when it's a secret. By giving the customer a chance to express dissatisfaction, this graceful letter gives the company a chance to uncover and rectify the problem and keep its customer.

Dear Ms. Ong:

You haven't used our [services, product] for a long time. Is there a problem we should know about?

Your business is very important to us, so we want to be sure we have lived up to your expectations.

Please let us know how we can serve you better. I've enclosed a reply card for your comments. I look forward to hearing from you and to being of service in the future.

Sincerely,

ENCL: reply card

2.11 *Asking for Letters of Recommendation*

Every time you make a big sale or do something special for your customers, ask them to write a brief letter describing what benefits they received from your product or service. Use this short letter as a guide.

"If you agree" lets customers know you won't be offended if they say no. (If customers won't write recommendations, often they will let you use their names. Letter 3.1 shows how to mention customers in a sales letter.)

Dear Manuela,

Your Christmas catalogue is a real winner! I'm especially pleased at the role that Allied Delivery could play in rushing your catalogues to your suburban stores in time for your deadline. We're proud that our extra effort paid off for you.

If you agree, when the dust has settled, I'd be grateful if you'd write us a short testimonial note we could use when we tell others about our emergency You-Want-It-When?! Service.

We look forward to the challenge and satisfaction of resolving your next delivery crisis.

Sincerely,

2.12   *Asking for Referrals*

This letter tells the reader exactly why a referral is so valuable and offers an incentive for supplying names.

Dear Lawrence:

You're worth $10 million to us.

That's because your good opinion is our most valuable advertising resource. Forget multi-million dollar TV campaigns and neon-covered dirigibles hanging over sports stadiums. We depend on *you*.

If you think Allied did a good job for you and could do the same good job for people you know, we'd like to hear about it. I've enclosed a reply card on which you can write the names and addresses of future Allied boosters. While we can't offer you the $10 million you deserve, we *will* extend your free maintenance agreement an additional month for each of your referrals who orders from Allied.

Thanks!

2.13   *Saying Thanks for Referral or Recommendation*

This letter thanks the customer for valuable referrals.

Dear Carolyn,

Thanks for your [valuable referrals, glowing recommendation]. I'm very grateful for your support and your confidence in Allied. We are always pushing to do the best for our customers, and we're proud that you are one of them.

Sincerely,

Chapter 3

Processing Orders, Payments, and Returns

Would that orders and payments were merely routine! Sadly, reams of correspondence are devoted to correcting irregularities in orders or payments. The following examples will help you respond to common situations in handling orders, payments, and returns.

3.1   *Expressing Appreciation for Order (with Delivery Information)*

Any letter regarding an order should begin with a note of appreciation for the customer's business.

Besides providing information about delivery dates, this letter lets the customer know her responsibilities for making sure the order proceeds smoothly.

RE: Your Order #221148

Dear Ms. Johnson:

On behalf of the Premier Medical Products Company, I would like to thank you for your order.

Please note that your purchase order number 221148, covering hospital beds and accessories, has been entered on Premier sales order numbers 3531, 3532, 3533, and 3534. I understand you are requesting staggered delivery beginning September 15 and continuing monthly through January of next year. Your architects must submit drawings and plans for the mounted accessories prior to September 1 to assure timely delivery. As soon as all manufacturing details have been finalized, I will send a formal acknowledgment confirming shipping dates.

Should you have any questions or need additional information, please contact Mr. Smith, our accessories manufacturing coordinator, or myself, at any time.

Thank you again for selecting Premier to supply your hospital's needs.

Sincerely,

Another note of appreciation for the customer's business brings this letter to a gracious close.

3.2   *Offering Final Confirmation of Order and Shipping Dates*

This follow-up confirms the details set forth in letter 3.1 and provides more specific information about shipping.

RE: Your Order #221148

Dear Ms. Johnson:

On behalf of the Premier Medical Products Company, I am pleased to inform you that all manufacturing details on your purchase order number 221148 have been finalized.

As the enclosed acknowledgment copies of Premier sales order numbers 3531, 3532, 3533, and 3534 indicate, the first part of your order is scheduled to load on a truck the week of September 15. As soon as more specific delivery information becomes available, Ms. Dawson of our shipping division will contact you personally. Each subsequent shipment will follow the first at 30-day intervals, as you requested.

Meanwhile, should you have any questions or need additional information, please contact Ms. Dawson or me at any time.

Once again, thank you for this very nice order.

Sincerely yours,

The writer again expresses the company's appreciation for the order.

ENCL: acknowledgment copies

3.3   *Requesting Additional Information to Process Order*

Missing information is a common problem in order processing. This form letter deals with frequently requested information in a clear, direct manner.

Dear Pimlico Customer:

Thank you for your purchase order dated March 9, 1998. Unfortunately, we are unable to process the order without the following information:

1. current catalogue numbers (catalogue enclosed)

2. telephone number and contact person's name

3. physical address for UPS delivery

4. address for billing

5. price approval for items being ordered

If you have questions or need assistance, please contact Customer Service at (800) 555-2277. Thank you for supplying the necessary information. We will process your order immediately upon receipt.

Sincerely,

3.4 *Responding to Query About Order*

Someone who is upset about an order that was never placed needs to be handled tactfully. That's why this letter begins by thanking the customer for writing.

The problem is introduced, along with the attempts the company has made to solve it.

Offering to provide overnight shipping at no cost shows the customer she matters—and is an incentive for her to respond quickly.

Don't hide when there's a problem! Follow this example and provide several options for communicating with your company.

Dear Ms. Neeland:

Thank you for your recent letter asking about the status of your order.

However, we have no record of your Zenon hardware order. We have tried to contact you by telephone but have been unable to reach you personally. We're sending this letter with instructions for placing your order.

We will expedite shipment as soon as we receive your order. We will also ship your product via overnight delivery at our expense. Orders must be prepaid; we accept checks (U.S. dollars and drawn on a U.S. bank), Visa, MasterCard, American Express, or domestic purchase orders (originals only).

Thank you for your interest in our products. If you have any questions or need further assistance, please contact our office at (800) 555-1231 or by fax at (504) 555-1243. My e-mail address is jdoe@zenon.com.

Sincerely,

3.5   *Returning Order (Special Offer Expired)*

This letter tackles a common situation—an order placed from an old catalogue whose prices are out-of-date or products are obsolete. Here, the company chooses to return the order rather than try to substitute other products for those no longer available.

Dear Ms. Martinez:

Thank you for your recent order for the Zenon Systems 5000 computer system and bundled software/CD-ROM drive.

Unfortunately, we are unable to process your request as it stands because the special offer expired more than two months ago and some of the software offered is no longer available. I have enclosed our most recent catalogue, which includes other offers that might be of interest.

Please accept our apologies for any inconvenience this may cause. We appreciate your understanding and your continued interest in Zenon Systems products. Please call if I can answer any questions about our current special offers.

Sincerely,

3.6   *Returning Check (No Order Enclosed)*

What to do when you receive a check and nothing else—or a check made out to the dry cleaners instead of your company? Return it with this letter, which gives the customer all the information needed to rectify the situation.

Dear Mr. Vincent:

Enclosed please find a check issued by you or your organization which we recently received. Unfortunately, the check was not accompanied by an order form or an invoice. Therefore, we're unable to apply the funds.

If you'd like to order a product, please mail the enclosed check with an order form or instruction letter to:

> Symantec Corporation
> Prepaid Order Processing
> 175 West Broadway
> Eugene, OR 97401

Please remember to include a street address for shipping and proof of ownership if you're ordering a product upgrade (i.e. copy of title page from user manual, program disk, customer ID number, or a copy of your original purchase receipt).

If you would like to make payment against an invoice, please mail the enclosed check with a copy of your invoice to:

> Symantec Corporation
> Attn: Accounts Payable
> 10210 Torero Avenue
> Cupertino, CA 95014

If you have any questions about this letter, please call Customer Service at (800) 555-1234 or (408) 555-1292.

Thank you.

Sincerely,

ENCL: check

3.7   *Explaining That Discounted Prices Do Not Apply to Customer's Order*

When the customer wants a service that is unreasonable, the response letter needs to be direct and firm. This letter explains the problem and clarifies the discount schedule that applies to this customer.

Attn: A. L. Reaman

Thank you for your recent blanket order #B11947-22. We have noticed that you are using our discounted prices based on the quantity you anticipate using throughout the length of the contract. Because quantity discounts are based on savings that occur when we do not have to break up prepackaged units, these discounts apply only on a per-shipment basis.

I have repriced the products on this order according to the pricing quoted, which we will honor for one year on the enclosed quote #Q8847.

For future orders, please note that quantity discounts will be offered as follows:

- Lots of 10 receive a 10 percent discount.

- Lots of 50 receive a 15 percent discount.

If you have any questions, please call me at (800) 555-1023, extension 222.

Sincerely,

3.8   *Informing Customer That a Product Is Not Available*

When you can't provide the product the customer wants, you can suggest an alternative, or send a letter such as this, returning the order. If the product is a big-ticket item, consider promising a personal call.

Dear Ms. Mettler:

Thank you for your recent order.

Unfortunately, Brabant Electronics does not offer the product you are requesting and therefore we are returning the order to you. I have enclosed a new catalogue of our products. If you would like to resubmit your order for a similar product, please make the changes and resend your order to Order Administration.

You can also retrieve a Brabant Electronics product list and information through our automated facsimile retrieval system by calling (800) 555-4311. Select Document #100 for a complete index of available documents. You will receive the information by fax within a few minutes of making your call.

If you should have further questions or need additional assistance, please contact Brabant directly at (800) 555-1123 or (206) 555-0118.

We apologize for any inconvenience this may cause and appreciate your support of Brabant Electronics.

Sincerely,

ENCL: returned order, catalogue

3.9   *Agreeing to Cancel Invoice on Undelivered Product*

Agreeing to a customer's request often requires an apology for the problem that prompted the request in the first place. This letter also begins with a statement of appreciation for the customer's letter.

Dear Mr. Mitchum:

Thank you for your recent letter. As you requested, I have rescinded the invoice for your order number 62115. The order shipped on February 26 because of a late delivery to our warehouse from the manufacturer. I understand that you needed delivery before the 15th of the month.

The order is currently on its way to you. Unfortunately, I cannot cancel delivery. When it arrives, simply refuse it and mark it "Return to Sender." We will cover all costs of shipping and your invoice will receive final cancellation.

I apologize for any inconvenience you experienced. Please know that this was an unusual circumstance; we hope to have an opportunity to give you our usually prompt, efficient service in the future.

Sincerely,

3.10   *Responding to Request to Cancel Service*

When the customer wants to sever your relationship, you need to accept that decision gracefully. This letter accepts the decision without question but adds that there may be a final invoice for outstanding charges.

The writer closes by expressing the hope that the company will be of service in the future.

Dear Cellular One Customer,

This is to confirm that we have received your 30-day written request to cancel your Cellular One service. Cellular telephone number [phone no.] for account number [acct. no.] was terminated as of [term. date].

You will be billed for any long distance or roaming charges as we receive tapes on them. You could receive a bill up to 60 to 90 days from now reflecting these charges. All current charges will be billed to you on the statement that you will receive approximately [date]. The amount currently owed as of today is $[amount].

If we can do anything else, let us know. We hope that we can be of service in the future.

Sincerely,

3.11   *Canceling Subscription and Requesting Verification of Instructions*

This form letter also accepts the customer's decision and asks the customer how to deal with a credit balance, promising prompt action.

Dear Mrs. Howell:

We received your request to discontinue delivery of *Xpressions* magazine. Your account is credited through [expiration].

Please verify your exact instructions regarding the credit which remains on your account. Return this entire letter in the envelope provided. Your response will receive our careful and prompt attention.

Please indicate your instructions for the credit balance:

❑ Continue to provide delivery through the expiration date.
❑ Discontinue delivery immediately and refund any remaining credit.
❑ Discontinue delivery immediately and transfer remaining credit to provide delivery to the person listed below:
❑ Transfer to:

Thank you for considering *Xpressions*.

Sincerely,

The ending expresses thanks for the customer's interest.

3.12   *Notifying Subscriber of Delivery Cancellation*

Rather than simply suggest that someday the customer might want to subscribe again, this letter provides specific information about how to renew a canceled subscription.

Dear Mr. Stuber:

This letter is to confirm that your Sunday-only subscription to the *Deseret News* has been canceled and your payment was credited to your account. As of the above date, your account (No. D33299) shows a zero balance.

We appreciate the opportunity we had to deliver the *Deseret News* to you, and we are sorry you have decided not to subscribe at the present time. If you decide to once again invite the *Deseret News* into your home, please call me, toll free, at (800) 555-0012, extension 3322. We hope to hear from you again soon.

Yours sincerely,

3.13   *Requesting Information About Returned Merchandise*

Opening acknowledges the return and describes the problem.

The request for more information is simple and direct, so the writer won't have to go back and ask again. Providing the return number as well as phone and fax numbers ensures the reader will reply promptly.

Dear Mr. Barnes:

Thank you for selecting a Symantec product.

Recently, we received a returned product from you. We were unable to locate any written instructions within the package.

In order to process this return in a timely manner, we need additional information. Please complete the enclosed form or contact our Order Administration Department at (800) 555-1029 to provide the information over the phone. You may also fax the paperwork to (800) 555-1103.

Please refer to RMA number SC-22431-44.

I look forward to hearing from you soon.

Sincerely,

ENCL: form

3.14 *Authorizing Supplier to Accept Returned Merchandise*

This letter grants the supplier's request but politely asks for more information.

> Dear Mr. Whitaker:
>
> Thank you for your inquiry about returning our products sent to you by your customers. This letter serves as authorization to return the following Zenon products:
>
> - Zenon Systems 5000
>
> - Zenon 2509x
>
> The return-of-merchandise authorization form enclosed requires only a few brief notes from you to enable us to process the return and apply the appropriate credit to your account. We especially appreciate knowing the reason for the return, as this helps us—and you—anticipate future problems and deal with them before they happen.
>
> The form also includes labels for you to apply to the shipping boxes. Just call UPS when you're ready for them to be picked up. If you have any questions at all, please feel free to contact Susan Farris at (502) 555-1094.
>
> Sincerely,
>
>
>
> ENCL: form

This paragraph reassures the reader that completing the form will be simple and extends appreciation for his cooperation.

Additional directions are specific and steer the reader through the task.

3.15 *Informing Customer Return Request Has Expired*

This form letter anticipates a problem before it arises. Its no-nonsense tone suggests there will be no compromise. For a more personal approach, include a note of appreciation or an acknowledgment that not having returned the product meant the customer was satisfied after all.

> Dear Mr. Lyle:
>
> On [date] we issued a return merchandise authorization (RMA) number. This number has been in effect more than 50 days without return of a product. As per arrangement with your Symantec distribution sales manager, this RMA has been canceled effective [cancellation date].
>
> Any product returned against this RMA number will be refused and returned to you at your expense. If you have any questions, please contact your distribution sales manager.
>
> Thank you,

Chapter 4

Handling Credit and Payment Problems

So many things can go wrong between the time an order is placed and sent and the payment received and processed that it's impossible to provide examples for every situation. The examples in this chapter represent the most common credit and payment situations. The key word in all of these letters is courtesy, and there are three basic elements:

1. thanking the customer for the order or payment

2. explaining the problem in nonjudgmental language

3. prescribing a clear action that can resolve the issue

Of course, this kind of letter should always include a telephone or fax number so the customer can contact you immediately about the problem.

When appeals for payment are ignored and an account begins to edge toward delinquency, a well-written letter can be a very effective weapon. The collection letters in this chapter progress from friendly reminders to notices that you are forwarding the past-due account to an agency or attorney. While they are always polite and straightforward, these letters tend to become a good deal more blunt as time goes along.

Granting credit is never a risk-free proposition. The key is to be able to determine who really is a good risk, and to handle those accounts in an intelligent, professional manner. For more information on how to do so, see *Credit and Collection Letters Ready to Go* by Ed Halloran (NTC Business Books). It reviews every step in establishing a client's creditworthiness and preventing or solving payment problems.

4.1   *Informing Customer That Postdated Checks Cannot Be Accepted*

Letter opens by thanking customer for the check.

When you say *no,* provide a real explanation. Instead of saying "Company policy dictates …" the writer tells exactly why postdated checks are no longer accepted.

The letter clearly states that this is an exception and the policy will be enforced in the future.

The closing calls attention to the benefit of enforcing this policy: keeping prices down.

Dear Mr. Ellison:

Thank you for your check in payment of our invoice No. 22231. We note that you have chosen to postdate this payment.

In the past, we have accommodated this practice, but due to fees charged by banking institutions for processing this kind of payment, we will no longer be able to honor postdated checks.

We will, in this instance, apply your payment on the requested date. However, in the future, your checks must be mailed to us with a current, cashable date.

The savings realized by our new procedure will ensure our ability to maintain the lowest possible costs for our customers. We appreciate your cooperation.

Best regards,

4.2   *Explaining That Customer Payment Was Incomplete*

Rather than cash the customer's first check and invoice the balance, this company returns the check and asks her to send the correct amount.

Letter notes that an attempt was made to reach the customer by telephone.

All three paragraphs provide precise instructions for the customer to follow.

Dear Ms. Jenkins:

Thank you for your order. Unfortunately, as the payment amount included doesn't completely cover the cost of the order we are returning the order with your check. Payment must include the amount of the product, shipping and handling ($10 for the first package and $5 for each additional package), and the appropriate sales tax for your state.

We have tried to contact you by telephone and have been unable to reach you. If you would like to resubmit your order, please include the enclosed order form with the correct amount and we will promptly fill your order.

Please include a _____ ss and the disk size you prefer, if this applic_____ e any questions regarding the pric-_____ onal assistance, please contact our _____ 5-0112.

_____ support of our products.

4.3   Re_____

The problem is explained in nonjudgmental language.

Telling the customer his order is ready to go encourages him to respond promptly.

De_____

_____ ver, since all orders must be p_____ rder because the accom-panyi_____

W_____ o ship, awaiting return of the _____

If y_____ nal assistance, please contact _____ at (550) 555-2911.

Than_____ y.

Sincerely,

ENCL: check

4.4   *Requesting Different Credit Card or Payment Method*

Besides providing several payment alternatives, this letter reassures the customer that this is a minor glitch that will not delay his order.

Dear Mr. Jorgensen:

Thank you for your recent order for Zenon products.

Unfortunately, we are unable to process your order on the Discover card. We are able to accept orders on Visa, MasterCard, or American Express. We have tried to reach you by telephone but have been unable to contact you personally.

In order to expedite your order, please call Customer Service at (800) 555-4319 or Prepaid Order Processing at (800) 555-1238, and place your order on one of the above credit cards. Mention order number 65-9938 to further simplify the process. We have kept your order on record and can ship as soon as we receive your payment information.

You may also choose to send payment by mail (check or money order in U.S. funds) to Prepaid Order Processing at the address below.

If you have any questions or need further assistance, please call Customer Service directly.

Thank you for your understanding and your continued interest in Zenon.

Sincerely,

4.5   *Explaining That Credit Card Was Not Accepted*

When a customer's credit card is not approved, the letter explaining the problem needs to carefully avoid any hint that the customer is at fault. This letter deftly skirts the question of exceeded credit limits by suggesting that the number might have been recorded incorrectly and asking the customer for verification.

Dear Ms. Washington:

Thank you for your recent order.

Unfortunately, during our bank transmission, your credit card number was not accepted. We have tried to reach you by telephone and have been unable to contact you personally. Please verify the number and expiration date in case we processed your number incorrectly. According to our records, your number is: 0123-4567-8900-0000, expiring June 2001.

In order to expedite your request, please call Customer Service at (800) 555-3210 to provide the correct number. You may also mail your order and payment directly to our order processing department at the address below.

If you have any questions or need additional assistance, please contact us by phone, or fax to (716) 555-2094.

Sincerely,

4.6   *Requesting New Payment (Follow-Up to Letter 4.5)*

This follow-up to letter 4.5 repeats the original request, continues to provide a multitude of payment options, and specifies a deadline after which the order will be canceled.

Dear Ms. Washington:

We appreciate your order, dated June 15. On June 21 we sent a letter notifying you that our bank did not approve your credit card. We are writing again to let you know that we still show your order as pending.

The credit card number we have on file for you is 0123-4567-8900-0000, expiration date June 2001. The price of the widget is $56.00; the shipping and handling charge is $8.00; tax is $3.92. Your total is $67.92.

If the above payment information is not correct, please make the necessary changes when resubmitting your order. We will accept payment by check or money order, or by Visa, American Express, or MasterCard. If you are responding by mail, please include this letter with your payment. You may also call us directly at (800) 555-3211. Please mention this letter when you call.

If we have not heard from you within 30 days, we will assume you no longer want this product and your order will be canceled.

Sincerely,

4.7   *Following Up to Verify an Adjustment Was Made*

Making credit adjustments is a routine procedure that many companies handle with straightforward form letters like this one.

Dear Cellular One Client,

This is to verify that the adjustment you requested was applied to your cellular account, [acct. no.] on [adj. date]. The total amount of the adjustment is $[adj. amt.], and will appear on your next month's invoice.

The amount of the credit will either be subtracted from the total monthly activity next month (if you pay this month's bill in full) or it will appear both as a balance forward *and* a credit, which will cancel each other out (if you subtract the credit amount from this month's invoice).

In either case, the amount due will be correct.

If you need any further assistance, or have any other questions, please give us a call!

Sincerely,

4.8   *Approving Credit Application*

This letter from an art supply store extends credit to a freelance commercial artist. It clearly states the store's credit terms and the customer's payment obligations. Showing gratitude for the customer's business is good manners—and helps build a relationship.

Dear Ms. Fong:

It is with great pleasure that I write to inform you that your application for a credit line has been approved. We've opened a revolving account for you with a limit of $500.

You will be billed monthly for all outstanding balances at an annualized rate of 12 percent. Your monthly invoice will be sent on the last day of the month, and a minimum payment is due within 21 calendar days of the date of the invoice. We require a minimum of 3 percent of the unpaid balance for amounts in excess of $15. Balances of less than $15 must be paid in full. Interest charges will be waived for the month billed if you pay your entire balance in full by the due date. This grace period should prove to be extremely helpful!

Thank you very much for choosing us as your supplier. We look forward to serving you for many years to come.

Sincerely,

P.S. I've enclosed a copy of our statement of terms and conditions.

4.9   *Approving Partial Credit*

This letter informs the vice president of manufacturing that her company does not qualify for the full amount of credit it has requested.

The company extends a "step-down" offer that lets the manufacturer complete its run.

Dear Ms. Smythe:

Thank you very much for your recent application to purchase $50,000 worth of widgets on credit from us. After a careful evaluation of the information you provided to us, we have concluded that we are unable to extend credit for the full amount.

However, you have qualified for $35,000 worth of credit under the terms and conditions in our standard contract. So, a down payment of $15,000 would enable you to acquire the full amount of widgets you'll need in order to complete your planned manufacturing run.

I've enclosed a revised contract that reflects the terms and conditions I've outlined in this letter. When we've received a signed contract and your down payment, we'll make and ship your widgets.

A look to the future ends this letter on a positive note.

I hope we'll be able to serve you for a long time to come.

Sincerely,

ENCL: contract

4.10   *Explaining That Credit Has Been Denied*

This letter offers a gracious thank-you before the bad news.

Writer reminds the customer he can still do business with the company and includes a positive statement about the future.

Dear Mr. Tomlinson:

Thank you for your recent application for credit. We regret to inform you that you don't qualify for a charge account at this time.

However, we believe that our high-quality products, first-rate customer service, and competitive pricing will make it well worth your while to do business with us on a cash basis, and we look forward to serving you.

Thank you very much for thinking of us.

Sincerely,

4.11   *Sending E-Mails and Faxes to the Moderately Late Customer*

Never demand payment via electronic transmission. It's too easy for your message to reach someone other than the debtor, and third-party notification is illegal and unethical. However, if your mailed invoices and reminder calls aren't getting you anywhere, try sending these electronic quickies via fax or e-mail.

Notice that none of these messages refers directly to the uncollected debt. Each is a friendly, face-saving letter.

If you get no response, try sending a message outside the debtor's normal business hours so it's waiting when he gets in the next morning.

If these communications still receive no response, it's time to return to regular collection letters.

Dear Mr. Jones:

I haven't heard from you lately, and I'd welcome the opportunity to talk with you. Please call me today. Thanks.

Sincerely,

or

Dear Mr. Jones:

"Telephone Tag" is no fun! I've been unable to get through to you for some time now, and I really need to talk to you. I'll be available from _____ to _____ today and tomorrow, and I've left express orders to route your call right through to me.

Sincerely,

or

Dear Mr. Jones:

An urgent problem has arisen concerning your order, and I need to speak with you as soon as possible. If I'm not in the office when you call, my pager number is _____.

I'm sending this electronically because I've been unable to get through to you on the phone.

Awaiting your call,

4.12   *Collecting from the Moderately Late Overseas Customer*

Several factors complicate overseas collection. Time differences and mail delays can hamper even willing debtors, as this letter points out. Also, some cultures have a more malleable view of time—and it's unlikely they will change without gentle encouragement.

This letter stresses the importance of timely payments. When it's clear an overseas customer is experiencing payment problems, call a translator—even if you are reasonably proficient in the language of the country.

Dear Ms. Baring-Crosse:

The mails can be slow, and we're certain your payment is on its way to us. If it is, please disregard this reminder.

We greatly value our business relationships, and hope to continue serving you. In order to do so, timely payments are a must, as our domestic suppliers bill us promptly for the goods and services they provide to us.

We look forward to receiving your payment soon. A copy of our invoice is enclosed for your records.

Cordially,

4.13   *Collecting from the Moderately Late Customer*

Depending on the size of your business, you may elect to begin sending collection letters when a customer is more than a week past due. This letter strikes an "I mean it" tone to tell the customer you are concerned about the problem and want payment immediately.

Re: Account #_____

Balance Due: $_____

Minimum Payment: $_____

Dear Ms. Zerlin:

YOUR ACCOUNT IS SERIOUSLY PAST DUE! You have not sent us the previous month's payment, and in a short time, another monthly payment will be due.

While we appreciate your business, we find your failure to communicate with us disquieting. Please be advised that we cannot consider extending additional credit to you until you've paid off your past due balance.

Please send us your check in the amount of $_____ today, or call our office to make payment arrangements.

Thank you.

Sincerely,

4.14   *Collecting from the Seriously Late Customer*

This firm letter does not include a minimum payment amount so the debtor will see the full amount due and realize why you are about to close the account. At this point, your letters should have lost their friendly tone. Keep your words within the boundaries of good taste. Don't threaten and don't use abusive language.

Account #_____

Balance due: $_____

Dear Ms. Lemmon:

   Your account is seriously past due, and your failure to contact us leaves us no choice but to close your account, effective immediately.

   We are willing to work with you, but in order to do so, we need to talk with you.

   Please call our office today.

   Thank you.

Sincerely,

4.15   *Writing the Closed-Account Letter*

Cut off anyone who is stiffing you! This letter stressing that the writer is willing to work with the customer to resolve the problem should encourage the customer to pick up the phone.

Re: Account #_____

Past Due Balance: $_____

Dear Mr. Sullivan:

   We were recently forced to close your account with us because you have not made any payments since _____, and you have also failed to contact our office.

   If you are experiencing financial difficulties, we can work out a payment schedule that will enable you to deal with meeting your obligations. In order to do so, however, we need to know what problems you're facing, so we can work together to resolve them.

   Please call us today.

   Thank you.

Sincerely,

4.16   *Writing the Lump-Sum Payment Letter*

Offering a lump-sum settlement creates a win-win situation. The debtor's balance will drop significantly, and the company will be paid. Determine what you are willing to settle for, and tell your customer. This is a good tactic to use with a customer who may file bankruptcy. Better to be paid a significant lump sum instead of a few cents on the dollar.

Account #_____

Balance Due: $_____

Re: Cleaning the slate

Dear Mr. Sullivan:

You have an opportunity to put your obligation to us behind you once and for all by sending us a lump-sum payment of $_____ to arrive not later than _____. As your current balance due is $_____, this one-time offer represents a savings to you of $_____.

When your check clears, we will send you a final statement, marked PAID IN FULL.

We're certain that if you weigh the alternatives, which may include legal action, you'll find this to be a very attractive opportunity for you to put this debt behind you.

If we haven't received your lump-sum payment by the due date, the balance due will revert to the full amount, and additional late fees and/or interest charges, as allowed under the terms of our original agreement, will increase the amount you owe.

We suggest that you avail yourself of this opportunity today.

Sincerely,

4.17   *Responding to Lump-Sum Payment Offer*

If your customer offers a lump-sum payment first, or makes a counter-offer, send a letter like this to confirm the agreement.

Account #_____

Balance Due: $_____

Dear Ms. Thackeray:

We have received your offer to settle this account by making a lump-sum payment of $_____. We're willing to accept this amount provided we receive the money not later than _____. Otherwise, the balance due will revert to the full amount, and additional charges may also apply.

When your check clears, we will send you a final statement marked PAID IN FULL.

Thank you.

Sincerely,

4.18   *Rejecting Lump-Sum Payment Offer and Proposing Payment Plan*

This letter rejects the lump-sum payment offer but still leaves a door open by offering a payment plan.

Account #_____

Balance Due: $_____

Dear Mr. Podgorski:

Thank you for your offer to settle this account for $_____. While we are unable to agree to your proposal, we are willing to work with you.

Our original settlement figure of $_____ remains firm. However, we are willing to set up a payment plan that will enable you to satisfy this obligation. Please send us a down payment of $_____ to arrive not later than _____. After that, we will accept monthly payments in the amount of $_____, provided your payments reach us by the first of the month.

If you don't accept this offer, or having accepted it, fail to keep the arrangements, the debt will revert to the original balance due, plus any applicable interest charges, late fees, etc.

Sincerely,

4.19 *Responding to Payment Plan Proposal*

This letter confirms the details of the proposal and clarifies the consequences of not living up to the agreement. Both you and the debtor should sign a standard promissory note that confirms the settlement figure.

Account #_____

Balance Due: $_____

Dear Ms. Zedko:

We are in receipt of your offer to settle this account for $_____ not later than _____. You have offered a down payment of $_____ and monthly payments of $_____ until the settlement figure is reached.

We are willing to accept your offer, provided you meet your proposed payment schedule. Failure to do so will result in the balance due reverting to the full amount plus any applicable interest charges and/or late fees.

When you've met the terms of this agreement, we'll send you a final statement indicating that the balance has been paid in full.

Thank you.

Sincerely,

4.20 *Notifying Customer of Intent to Forward Account to Collection*

If no results are forthcoming, it's time to charge off the account and send it out. By telling the customer this stage is near, the writer gives him one last chance to make good.

Account # _____

Balance Due: $_____

Subject: FINAL NOTICE

Dear Mr. Jones:

If you do not send us the full amount due or if you fail to contact this office by _____ to make acceptable payment arrangements, this account will either be turned over to a collection agency or sent out for legal action with no further communication from this office.

Please take the time to resolve this matter today.

Sincerely,

4.21   *Notifying Customer That Account Has Been Forwarded to Collection*

This letter makes clear that negotiations are over and there is nothing more to do than send the account to an agency or attorney.

Account #_____

Balance Due: $_____

Dear Mr. Jones:

Your account has been charged off and has been forwarded to [our attorney, an agency] for immediate action.

Sincerely,

Announcing Price Increases, Policy and Personnel Changes, Delays, and Cancellations

Change is good. Maybe—if your customers aren't surprised, confused, inconvenienced, or convinced you're trying to put something over on them. Announce changes very clearly. Be sure you've got your reader's attention. (Before you mutter about "those @#* people who don't read their mail," think about all the announcements and notices you've gotten and didn't read until it was too late.)

Sometimes the change you have to announce—a price increase, a delay, a policy change—appears to let your customers down. When that is the case, tell them as far in advance as possible. Never, *never* procrastinate when it comes to bad news. Acknowledge it quickly, so your customers can plan accordingly. The manufacturer who knows two weeks ahead that important components will be late can rearrange production activities and keep his or her plant running smoothly. The manufacturer who learns the day before the shipment is expected that it will be two weeks late will have a harder time rescheduling—and will be unlikely to forgive the supplier for the delay!

5.1 *Announcing Price Increase*

Is it really a price increase if the operating cost is lower than ever? By offering these surprising comparisons, this letter puts the price increase in a context the customer can understand and probably accept.

Dear Ms. Fenton:

How can a price increase save you money?

When Allied began manufacturing its famous Turbo-Lamp in 1943, a phone call was a nickel, a gallon of milk was 36¢, and the Turbo-Lamp gave you 400 hours of light for .0010¢ per hour.

Today a phone call costs 20¢ (a 300 percent increase), a gallon of milk costs $3.08 (a 755 percent increase) and the Turbo-Lamp now gives you 5,000 hours of light at a cost of .0005¢ per hour—a 50 percent price *decrease*!

Allied is enormously proud of the contribution the Turbo-Lamp has made to the exploration of our planet. We look forward to our challenging role in the forthcoming Mars expedition and in the colonization of the solar system.

Sincerely,

5.2   *Announcing Price Increase*

Opening hooks the reader's interest.

Revealing the issues behind the decision lets the company position the increase as a benefit—maintaining the high quality customers rely on.

Increasing discount rewards customer for loyalty and closes the letter on a positive point.

Dear Mr. Garcia:

Did we make the right decision? Your next order will tell us.

When Allied heard about the big price increases in the raw materials that go into our top-of-the-line models, we had a big decision to make:

- Should we maintain our current prices by reducing quality?

- Or should we maintain our quality, even if it meant raising prices?

We didn't agonize for long. We realized that without our reputation for excellence, we wouldn't keep you as our customer. That's why, <u>very reluctantly</u>, we have had to raise our prices 6 percent across the board.

To take some of the sting out of this move, we are increasing your Preferred Customer discount on quantity orders to 9.5 percent.

Sincerely,

5.3   *Announcing Price Increase*

Underlined headings let the reader immediately grasp the purpose of the letter.

The reason for the increase is carefully explained.

Business practices are tied to the company's ability to contain other prices.

News of a new product line closes letter on a positive note and encourages reader to open the catalogue.

Dear Mr. Lorenz:

Enclosed is our new price schedule for spring. We won't try to fool you. Some prices have gone up. But some have gone down.

<u>Which Prices Have Gone Up?</u> As you go through the list, you'll see the increases are principally for products made of wood or for ceramics shipped from Pacific Rim countries.

Quality lumber, as you may know, has nearly doubled in price during the last three years due to more careful harvesting of our precious national forests. Until now, many of our suppliers were able to keep prices down by drawing on their backlog of aging woods. But now the supply is exhausted and they must pass the price increases on to us and to you. The higher ceramic prices reflect larger import duties levied by the U.S. government, plus an increased standard of living for the talented artisans who produce these exquisite pieces.

<u>Which Prices Have Gone Down?</u> The news isn't all bad. We're proud that careful purchasing has allowed us to hold the line on our fine linens, and an improved warehousing system has cut the handling costs on our extensive collection of quality flatware and kitchenware.

And we are very enthusiastic about our expanded line of exciting party supplies. You can check them out on page 75.

We're eager for your reactions.

Sincerely,

ENCL: price schedule

5.4   *Announcing Policy Change*

When something is new or different, tell your readers clearly. Bold heading captures attention, tells readers why they must read this letter.

Bold type highlights key phrases; underlined sentences make the three options hard to miss. Simple instructions enable the customer to act immediately.

IMPORTANT NOTICE

YOU MUST CHOOSE ONE OF THREE OPTIONS.

Dear Ms. Letterman:

You are currently enrolled in Sky-Dish's Optional Maintenance Plan. For a standard monthly fee, the plan covers repairs and replacement of all parts and cables, at no additional cost to you.

Beginning June 1, the price of this plan will increase from $.75 to $.95 per month. The increase will appear in your July bill, retroactive to June 1st.

You have three options:

1. Keep the Optional Sky-Dish Maintenance Plan you currently have. If this is your choice, don't do anything. We'll simply bill you at the new rate of $.95 per month.

2. Upgrade to our Sky-Dish Enhanced Maintenance Service for just $2.00 a month. Complete details are in the enclosed brochure. To subscribe, call toll free (800) 000-0000.

3. Discontinue your current plan at no charge. To discontinue, call toll free (800) 000-0000.

Please read the enclosed information carefully, including terms and conditions. Whatever your choice, we are happy to serve you.

Sincerely,

ENCL: brochure

5.5   *Announcing New Policy*

Headline announces policy change.

The change and the date it is effective are clearly explained.

Indicating reluctance acknowledges customer relationship, asks for understanding from long-term customers.

Dear Mr. McClave:

CHANGE IN BILLING PROCEDURES

Starting March 15, Allied will begin charging a 5 percent monthly carrying fee on all balances more than 60 days past due.

We have been very reluctant to take this step, especially since many of our accounts have been with us for quite a few years. We have been through good and bad economic times together, so it was especially difficult for us to decide to make this change.

As always, we are very willing to work with our clients whenever problems arise.

Sincerely,

5.6   *Announcing New Policy*

Headline commands attention, makes sure change won't be overlooked.

This list makes it easy for the reader to see what will and will not be accepted.

This paragraph tells why the change was necessary.

An apology is followed by a positive look toward the future.

NOTICE

CHANGE IN TRADE-IN POLICY

Dear Ms. Sargis:

Starting February 15th, the items Allied can accept as trade-ins for recycling will change as follows:

NO LONGER ACCEPTED

- model C101-B

- model X133-Z

- model Y222

STILL ACCEPTED

- all Model B101's

- all jet models

We deeply regret any inconvenience this change will cause you. Unfortunately, the recycler we have used for the past ten years is no longer able to accept these parts at his current location. He is seeking new facilities and also exploring new processes to render these parts ecologically harmless.

If we are able to make new arrangements, we will let you know immediately. In the meantime, we apologize. We felt really good about being able to offer this valuable service and hope we can do so again.

Sincerely,

5.7   *Announcing Merger and Company Name Change*

When the announcement is big, make it easy for your readers to understand what the news means to them. Figure out what they need to know and what they want to know.

Underlined sections answer the reader's questions about changes triggered by the merger and new name.

Bullets help the reader digest important points without feeling overwhelmed by new information.

Dear Account Holder:

As you may have heard, Ulysses Bank is becoming part of First Priam Bank. Two enclosed booklets provide important information about some of the changes, and within the week you'll receive a comprehensive catalogue of all First Priam's financial services. In the meantime, you probably want to know exactly what these changes will mean to *you*:

What will be the same?

- Your Ulysses accounts and services are unaffected.

- You can continue to use your Ulysses checkbooks, passbooks, loan payment coupons, etc. (Replacements with the First Priam Bank insignia will be issued when you need new ones.)

- You can continue to bank at your familiar Ulysses Bank branches. (First Priam signs will begin to appear on Ulysses branches in your neighborhood and throughout the state.)

What will be different?

- Starting December 10, you can also use any of First Priam's 1,300 branches from Baltimore to Key West.

- Many fees will now be lower. (Check the enclosed schedule.)

- You'll also find many more options to avoid paying fees.

We know you may have questions during the coming weeks. Please feel free to visit us any time at any location, or call our toll-free information line at (800) 000-0000. We'll be pleased to hear from you.

Sincerely,

P.S. Please keep these two booklets, plus the catalogue you'll get next week, for future reference.

5.8   *Announcing Personnel Changes*

When announcing a long list of changes, follow this writer's lead and send along Rolodex cards or a revised phone directory readers can file for quick reference.

> Dear Ms. Cavin:
>
> Here are six Rolodex cards that will bring you up-to-date on the recent personnel shifts at Allied.
>
> We've had a lot of changes. George Formby, our new products director for the past eleven years, is retiring as of June 5th, and Jack Hulbert will be taking over that department. To replace Jack, Jessie Matthews is stepping up to plastic lab manager, and her longtime assistant, Cecily Courtneidge, will ably fill her shoes in production. Our new lab coordinator is an enterprising (relative) youngster, Evelyn Laye, who has spent the last eight years as a vice president with J. B. Cochran Products.
>
> Since you can't tell the players without a scorecard, we've listed everyone's new titles and extensions on the enclosed phone directory cards. Just snap the cards in place and give us a call.
>
> Sincerely,
>
>
> ENCL: phone directory cards

5.9   *Announcing Personnel Changes*

If this partner has left under a cloud, the letter needn't say more. Otherwise, the writer should provide some reason, such as ill health or a decision to join a monastery or keep bees. If he has gone to another firm, the letter should say so with as much or as little enthusiasm and thanks as necessary.

> Dear Mr. O'Brien:
>
> Ezra Winslow has left Langdon, Keaton, Chaplin, and Chase as of November 16th, and is no longer a partner with our firm.
>
> Mr. Winslow's accounts are being assigned to the remaining partners and you will hear from either Mr. Keaton or myself within a few days to make the transition as seamless as possible. We look forward to a continuing and productive collaboration.
>
> Sincerely,

5.10   *Announcing a Death*

This letter announces a death and tells customers who to contact instead.

> Dear Allied Customer:
>
> It is with great regret that we announce the sudden death on April 21 of Rosa Chan, a valued and highly esteemed colleague at Allied.
>
> Ms. Chan has been chief auditor in our Wichita office for the past four years. Her cheerfulness, energy, and skill will be sorely missed by her many friends at Allied and in the business community.
>
> For the time being, Ms. Chan's duties will be taken over by Denis Ducastel, assistant to the president. Please direct your inquiries to Mr. Ducastel at ext. 808.
>
> Sincerely,

5.11   *Explaining Delays and Cancellations*

A typical delay or cancellation letter should follow this format. Multiple sample phrases are listed beneath each directive.

> **Start by apologizing:**
> *Your order is going to be late and we apologize!*
> *Your calls to Allied have been going unanswered and we apologize!*
> *Your Allied billing has become a victim of computer-age gremlins. We apologize for any inconvenience that you are experiencing!*
> *We want to apologize for any service delays you may be having due to Hurricane Griselda.*
> **Offer some compensation:**
> *To get your order to you as quickly as possible, we are shipping it by air at our own expense.*
> *We are eager to keep you as a customer and will refund your payment for this order. Enclosed is our check for $780.60.*
> *We will credit your account for $224.05 (our invoice # 831106), plus an additional $50.00 as our thanks to you for staying with us through this difficult time.*
> *We will reimburse you for any additional expenses you have directly incurred for replacements due to this problem. Just send me photocopies of your bills.*
> *Will you accept the enclosed vouchers for $100 credit toward future orders?*

Explain problem (Optional):

As you may be aware, a strike was called against one of our major suppliers by Amalgamated Workers on June 20. Because of this unfortunate dispute, service was suspended from June 23 to July 5 at our Texas plant, delaying shipments two weeks. This means we temporarily cannot offer our full range of toasters.

As you may be aware, the recent severe storms along the east coast of the United States have caused numerous delays in air, rail, and trucking shipments. Allied is doing everything possible to overcome these delays and restore your services. Our local staff has volunteered to work 80 hours a week during the crisis, and we've flown in sixteen additional workers from other parts of the country.

Our computer system was designed to serve a customer base of 10,000. That was fine when we started in 1981 with just 30 customers, but, because of the support of people like you, Allied has surpassed that capacity. Last October we switched to a system that should serve you well, well into the twenty-first century. Unfortunately, any big change like this can bring tremendously frustrating, if temporary, problems.

Explain how problem will be solved (Optional):

We are literally working day and night with our supplier to resolve this problem.

On December 5, our new reactor went on line, which should get us back to normal by next week.

We expect to restore full service within the next few days.

Now that the computer problem has been resolved, our warehouse people are working day and night to get your back orders to you. Right now, we anticipate being completely back on schedule by March 12th.

Provide background (Optional):

We would like to give you some background on the disagreement that caused this stop-work action. [Provide an objective, very brief account of the events and management's efforts to resolve the issues, such as: "The union felt the scheduling limits set by a federal court could not be implemented in time for the deadline without undue hardship on union members." Don't make anyone out to be the bad guy. Maintain a neutral and regretful tone.]

Close on a positive note:

Our biggest concern is to resolve the problem and fill your orders as quickly as possible. Again, we apologize for these problems. Thank you for bearing with us through these difficult days. We value you!

Sincerely,

Chapter 6

Resolving Complaints and Acknowledging Mistakes

One angry or unhappy customer is like a ticking time bomb. Numerous surveys indicate that he or she will tell at least a half dozen people about your failings (real or imagined) and each of those people will mention it to a half dozen more, and so on. Given human nature and mathematical progressions, your company can get a lot of bad publicity very quickly.

That's why it is important to keep your customers as happy as possible—or at least impressed with your fairness and concern. One way to do so is to respond promptly and graciously to all customer complaints. But be careful what you say and how you say it, or your letter may do more harm than good.

A national business magazine recently featured real examples of good and bad corporate responses to a customer's problem, a shipping delay that had cost the customer a bundle. Even though the "good" letter in the article went a lot further than the "bad" toward soothing the injured customer, it didn't go far enough. The writer of the "good" letter first made the reader read through three paragraphs—175 words—which listed all the reasons, legal and common practice, why the company was not required to help the customer. Finally, in paragraph four, the fuming reader reached the statement: "We value your business . . . therefore, I am offering $0,000 . . ."

How do you think the reader felt at this point? The writer certainly didn't intend to alienate a customer. After all, the bottom line (literally) was that the customer was going to be compensated for the loss. Shouldn't that be enough? Well, no.

The "good" example in the article followed the writer's train of thought instead of the customer's concerns. By the time the customer had read through all the reasons why the writer couldn't and shouldn't compensate the customer for the loss, the customer's goodwill toward the writer's company was probably at rock bottom and his or her blood pressure sky high. The writer's offer of compensation in the last paragraph came too late to prevent those feelings.

Put your customers' interests first. *Don't* list all the reasons the law doesn't require you to stand behind your product or service, and *then* say reluctantly that you will make good to keep the customer. Start out on the right foot:

Dear

   Here is our credit for $800 to help compensate you for your losses because your February 3 order was delayed in shipping. Even though our insurer refuses to cover any loss due to shipping delays, we know how crucial it is to you to get every Allied shipment on time. That's why we're willing to "eat" this expense. We want to show you how valuable you and your business are to us.

Then, if really necessary, go on to explain any background on the situation, what you are doing to prevent future problems, etc.

Acknowledging Mistakes—and Apologizing

Some writers are eager to deny responsibility for any problem because they fear their company may be sued. And it is true that a careless sentence may give your customer grounds for legal action against your company. For example, the following sentences admit to a potentially litigious responsibility:

> *We've very sorry our slippery floors caused you to fall and break your hip.*
>
> *Your mail-order catalogue did not get posted by the date specified in our contract because the sorted bags were mismarked and misplaced in the mailroom. We apologize for any inconvenience.*
>
> *The sales associate you spoke with misrepresented our company policy; we regret we cannot honor your request.*

However, you can be sympathetic without giving litigious clients real ammunition for a legal battle. A simple apology can show sympathy for the frustrations the customer has experienced that are neither your fault nor the customer's. In those situations, saying "I'm sorry" simply means "I'm sorry to hear you're having difficulty."

When your company *has* made a mistake, an apology is definitely in order. But apologizing doesn't mean groveling. To apologize gracefully, maintain the company's dignity as well as a respectful attitude toward the customer. If explanations are needed, provide them succinctly. Most customers won't be interested in excuses, but by briefly explaining the situation behind the problem you're apologizing for, you can sometimes win understanding.

This chapter offers a variety of ways to acknowledge a mistake, offer condolences or sympathy, and repair damage—all designed to help you maintain a good relationship with your customers in light of their complaints.

6.1   *Responding to Complaints*

Follow this model when it's time to reply to a customer with a complaint. (Keep in mind that some steps may not apply to specific products or services.) Multiple sample phrases are listed beneath each directive.

Express concern that the customer is unhappy (which is not an admission of fault).

We were very concerned to learn of your experience with our Zip-Master electric zipper.

Your report of problems with our DX-40 is of great concern to us.

React—Describe what you can and will do to help the customer.

Please use the enclosed prepaid express delivery form to return the parts to me. I will immediately issue you a full credit as soon as they arrive.

We have notified our local representative, Frances Dee, to contact you immediately about repairs or replacement.

Diagnose—Offer a possible explanation (not an excuse) for what happened, if this is appropriate.

Our quality control lab will conduct exhaustive tests to discover the cause of the problem. One possibility is that these components were affected by corrosion, due to exposure to salt air.

Sometimes when the peanut butter comes in contact with especially acidic jam, a chemical reaction occurs that causes a temporary whitening of the peanut butter. This doesn't affect the taste or quality in any way.

Remedy—Describe what you can and will do to prevent the problem from recurring.

All future shipments to your area will be hermetically sealed and shrink wrapped to deter contamination.

Our kitchen experts are currently working on a new peanut butter formulation, testing it with various jams. They want our Fluffy Nut to be as much a treat for the eye as it is for the taste buds.

Thank the customer for supporting your organization, as demonstrated by taking the time to report a problem.

Thank you for alerting us to this situation. We greatly appreciate your conscientiousness and depend upon customers like you to help us keep Allied the quality leader in the industry.

Letters like yours are extremely important to us. Your feedback is imperative if we are going to continue to grow and to satisfy your needs.

We are very grateful to customers like you who take the time to contact us. Your support is greatly appreciated.

Reward—Express your thanks with a coupon, discount, etc. (Optional)

Please accept the enclosed coupon for a complimentary pair of Zip-Master electric scissors.

We invite you to try our newest Fluffy Nut Sundae Sprinkles with our compliments. A jar is enclosed.

Sincerely,

ENCL: [whatever reward is]

6.2 *Responding to Complaints*

This letter starts with concern that the customer *perceives* a problem. That is different from admitting a problem exists.

Dear Ms. Pollux:

We were concerned to learn of your dissatisfaction with Allied's [name of product].

You said that [repeat complaint]. This [was, may have been] because [explanation]. We have notified our [director of quality control, shipping supervisor, district manager], who will be looking into the situation and may contact you with further questions.

Thank you for the cooperative spirit that prompted you to contact us. Please accept the enclosed adjustment with our apologies. We will try harder to make all your future Allied purchases completely satisfactory.

Sincerely,

ENCL: adjustment

6.3   *Responding to Complaints*

One of the best ways to disarm a complaint is to thank the customer for making it. Showing concern impresses the customer with your caring and commitment. Use this short, simple letter to follow up on a telephone call that ended in a resolution.

Dear Mr. Louie:

Thank you for calling me today about your [billing, service, shipping, etc.] problem. I understand your frustration and personally apologize on behalf of Allied for the difficulties you had in this situation.

To restate what we agreed, [describe solution]. I hope this resolution will help restore your confidence in Allied.

Please consider me your advocate if you have any future problems.

Sincerely,

6.4   *Responding to Complaint Arising from Customer Misunderstanding*

Any letter that has to tell the customer he or she was wrong needs to include a message of thanks. This letter shows appreciation as well as sympathy.

Even though the message is clear that the company was not at fault, the letter does not blame the customer or even say she misunderstood the situation. The explanation that delivery time is noted on the order form is the only suggestion that the information had been available to the customer.

Suggesting an alternative solution ensures the same mistake won't be made twice.

Dear Ms. Davis:

I appreciate your letter explaining your frustration at missing the Federal Express delivery of your order. I want to thank you for taking the time to write.

When you requested second-day delivery by Federal Express, you were automatically scheduled to receive your package no later than noon on January 29. Only priority next-day-air packages are guaranteed to arrive by 10 a.m., which is noted in the customer service guidelines on our order form.

For future reference, you can arrange to have the package left by signing a release form with Federal Express. That way you won't be required to miss work to wait for delivery. You can also specify that packages be delivered to your work address, if that would be more convenient.

Be assured that we are ready to work with you to make sure you get the service you want. Again, thank you for writing. If I can be of any further help, please call me at (303) 555-2298.

Sincerely yours,

6.5 *Responding to Unjustified Complaint*

Many problems arise because of a mistake the customer made—yet the customer feels it was your fault in some way. This letter tactfully explains the customer's and printer's responsibilities without assigning—or wrongly accepting—blame.

Sympathy is extended by pointing out that the company has been on the receiving end of the same problem.

Mentioning the signed proof copy reminds the client that she accepted responsibility for checking for errors.

Dear Ms. Kingsford:

We were concerned to receive your letter expressing your disappointment with the brochure we printed for you last week. It's all too common to find a typographical error only when it's in final printed form—no matter how many people have proofread it!

We sympathize with your frustration because we've experienced it with our own printed pieces. While we take every effort to produce flawless publications for our customers, we must rely on you to be the final approval.

The process of putting together a printed piece involves a great many steps and many people. Our part of that process requires us to prepare film from the mechanicals your artist provides; create proofs from the film for your final approval; make any changes that you specify after carefully proofreading the final proofs, making additional proofs if you require them; and print the job to your specifications.

When artwork is created by another party and not in our plant, we do not proofread the content; we check only for problems that might occur in printing, such as misplaced margins or improper crop marks.

The proof copy that you sign, approving the job for printing, emphasizes the need for careful proofreading for just this kind of situation. The only solution, at this stage, is to reprint if you feel the typographical error is too serious to let stand.

If you reprint, the cost will be reduced by about 27 percent because you have already incurred the basic set-up costs for film and plates. Please call me if you would like a precise quote on reprinting costs.

Thank you for your understanding. I look forward to hearing from you.

Sincerely,

6.6 *Explaining Possible Causes for Equipment Malfunction*

Following this letter's example and expressing concern about problems your customer is having with your product or services is one way to avoid either accepting or placing blame.

Although the engineering department believes this problem was caused by atmospheric conditions in the customer's plant, this letter takes an indirect approach. It offers assurances and various options for taking care of the problem.

Last paragraph is positive and reassuring.

Dear Mr. Sheldrake:

I was concerned to learn of the problems you have experienced with the high-speed drill assembly unit we installed for you in 1993. I am pleased to know the problems involve its appearance rather than its performance.

I have consulted with our engineering department about the corrosion of the casing. John Brye, our chief technical specialist, assures me that although it may look unsightly, the casing is the stopgap against corrosion of the more important inner mechanisms.

To correct the visual appearance, John suggests applying a coating of a rust-resistant paint, then a plastic resin-type coating. We could perform this for you in our factory, but you would lose valuable production time. John has readied the necessary materials and instructions for immediate shipment to your plant, if you'd prefer to handle it yourself. Just let me know what you decide.

The corrosion itself may be caused by severe temperature changes combined with high humidity. If you apply salt to your parking areas during freezing weather, some of the salinity may transfer to the air and worsen the reactions.

I look forward to hearing from you. As always, we're committed to giving you the best products along with the best service. Our support doesn't stop with the bill of sale.

Sincerely,

6.7   *Apologizing for Error in Company Advertising*

Presenting incorrect information in an advertisement can create big problems. This form letter apologizes for an incorrectly advertised price and explains how the company corrected the mistake.

Dear Santina's Customer:

Thank you for your letter regarding our mid-December sale advertisement. We appreciate the time you took to let us know of the error, and we sincerely apologize for your disappointment at not finding the sale item at the price that was advertised by mistake in last Sunday's newspaper.

As can so easily happen, a number was transposed—from the correct price of $52.95 to $25.95—which made a big difference! We immediately called the newspaper, which ran a corrected ad on Tuesday. Unfortunately, that wasn't enough to save several of our valued customers from a frustrating experience.

A coupon helps compensate the customer for his or her trouble.

We want to thank you for your patience and understanding. We care about your business, and we want your trips to Santina's to be fulfilling. Therefore, please accept the enclosed 10 percent off coupon for your next visit.

Sincerely,

ENCL: coupon

6.8   *Apologizing for Referring Bill to Collection Agency in Error*

There's no use explaining the situation behind this problem—it's much too serious to justify. This letter gets right down to the business of apologizing and telling how the problem has been corrected.

Dear Ms. Stenopoulos:

I am taking this opportunity to formally apologize to you for the mistake made on your account billing. Due to an error on our part, your gift subscription continued beyond the period ordered by the party giving you the gift. As a result, your account was placed for collection by mistake. We have cleared the outstanding balance on your account. Please accept our apology.

We have notified our collection agency and they have removed your name from their records. We have been assured that there will be no negative effect on your credit rating.

Please accept the enclosed gift as a token of our sincere regret for the inconvenience we have caused you.

Thank you for making us aware of the mistake we made in your billing. Please let me know if there is anything else I can do to make this right. My direct phone number is 555-2211.

Sincerely,

ENCL: gift

Chapter 7

Expressing Thanks and Congratulations

Any time you can sincerely say "Thank you," do so. Who should you thank? That's easy. Thank *everyone*: clients, prospective clients, suppliers, colleagues, subordinates, even superiors.

Thank customers for their orders, their cooperation, and their praise. A simple "thank you" on the back of a postcard or a Post-it Note attached to an order confirmation can prompt a smile and remind your customers of what a great company you have.

Thank those who have done something for you, even if they get paid for it, even if they weren't very good. That's good etiquette. Thank anyone who has done something extra or outstanding, even if it was "just my job." That's good business.

Praise excellence and acknowledge effort. Personalize. There are few things more devastating than laboring mightily and then getting a terse, impersonal thank-you form letter.

Mention what the reader did and describe your reaction. If you weren't there, describe what you have heard about it. If you heard only bad things, describe how important the job was and how you appreciate that it was done. Ignore your parents' adage that if you can't say something nice, don't say anything at all. Good or bad, a creative writer can find something positive to say about any event.

Warm, sincere, personal thank-you letters offer a higher eventual return than any other letter! But *never* begin a thank-you letter with the unfortunately common phrase: "I just wanted to take a moment to thank you for . . ." Although you don't mean it that way, it's insulting, implying that a moment is all the reader is worth.

And while you're writing, don't overlook the power of simple congratulations. Promotions, retirements, weddings, births, honors, awards—people love to be recognized for milestones and accomplishments. That's why a genuine letter of congratulations is worth more than all the advertising, direct-mail brochures, and fancy attention-getters. It shows you care, and helps customers and colleagues feel important.

The Thank-You Checklist

The letters in this chapter can help you get in the thank-you habit. But if you're stumped, this checklist can stimulate your thank-you gland. Use it to draft short but meaningful thank-you notes by the dozen! (Use the blank lines to customize the list to meet your own needs and clients.) Whenever you spot someone you could or should thank—as you go through your mail, after a phone call, or after a conference or important meeting—jot the person's name at the top of your form, check off the appropriate boxes, and fill in the blanks. Later you or your secretary can quickly craft these checklists into much appreciated thank-you notes or letters.

Dear _____

Thanks so much for

❏ helping with . . .

❏ participating in . . .

❏ contributing to . . .

❏ taking the time to . . .

❏ backing us up on . . .

❏ your extra effort to . . .

❏ meeting our deadline for . . .

❏ helping to make the project a big success.

❏ being such an important part of the winning team.

❏ _____

❏ _____

❏ _____

I really appreciate your

❏ hard work.

❏ extra effort.

❏ valuable contribution.

❏ taking time from your busy schedule.

❏ bailing us out when . . .

❏ always being there for us.

❏ valuable input and insights.

❏ unfailing support and encouragement.

❏ composure and cheerfulness when the going got rough.

❏ commitment and concern. No one could have worked harder.

❏ _____

❏ _____

❏ _____

You certainly

❏ increased my awareness of . . .

❏ expanded my view of . . .

❏ met all the difficulties with [energy, a cool head, a real understanding of the problems involved].

❏ were wonderful, terrific, and definitely on target.

❏ _____

❏ _____

❏ _____

In closing,

❏ it was a great success, and we couldn't have done it without you.

❏ everything went even better than I had dared hope.

❏ it was everything I hoped it would be.

❏ thanks for helping to make the project such a success.

❏ thanks for helping to bring it all together.

❏ we look forward to working with you again.

❏ _____

❏ _____

On behalf of Allied, my sincere appreciation for a job well done.

Sincerely,

7.1   *Thanking Customers for Their Business*

Send a simple note like this when it is appropriate: on your company's anniversary, when a customer reaches a milestone like five years of business, or on some other significant date.

Dear friends,

I glanced at my calendar this morning and realized it was only three years ago today that my partner and I launched Custom Mechanics in my garage at home. What a difference three years can make!

Today, Custom Mechanics has 54 highly trained professionals in three locations in the state. And we're getting ready to move into Wisconsin and Minnesota in January.

We couldn't have done it without your support and confidence. We felt it was time to stop and say thanks for being our customer!

Best regards,

7.2   *Thanking Customer Who Helped Out*

Dear John,

Your presentation at the Rotary Club was inspired—and inspirational. I know several members who walked away geared up for improving their business planning.

You've always been an important customer at Centech, and I knew that with your business acumen and experience you would have a lot to offer at the business development program. I want to thank you again for responding to my plea with such generosity.

Please be my guest for lunch the next time you're in town. I'm looking forward to a chance to talk with you further about your presentation. You gave me some very intriguing ideas!

Again, please accept my very sincere thanks.

With best regards,

This customer did the writer a favor—addressed his Rotary Club chapter. Whether they are simple or involved, gestures like these should be acknowledged promptly with a personal note, perhaps even handwritten.

7.3   *Thanking Customer for Comments and Providing Information*

Dear Mr. Farmer:

Thank you for taking the time to write about your pleasure in the *Growstarter* compound. We are always delighted to hear success stories such as yours, and we're particularly impressed with the results you've accomplished—85 pounds of tomatoes from one plant in a single day! That may be one for the record books!

You mentioned that you had less success with your harvest of green peppers. I checked with our resident botanist, Helen Channing, and she recommends that for your location and climate, you could add a pH neutralizer to the soil about a month before planting. Once sprouts appear, apply the *Growstarter* weekly instead of twice monthly for the first month, then follow the standard instructions.

I wish you luck with next year's harvest! And thank you again for writing. Your comments really mean a lot to us.

Yours sincerely,

As in this case, when a customer writes to report success with your products or services, always take time to say thank you.

This letter goes the extra mile by providing advice the customer can use for even better results.

7.4   *Thanking Customer for Letter Praising Employees*

When customers write to praise your employees, respond personally with a very appreciative note of thanks such as this one—and be sure to share the letter with those involved.

Dear Ms. Ikida:

Thank you so much for your wonderful letter! It's comments like yours that remind us why we at Grace Brothers enjoy coming to work. Though it may sound strange, we've sometimes had to work hard to keep up the sense of fun and enjoyment you experienced. We want both our employees and our customers to think of being at Grace Brothers as one of the day's highlights.

Thank you for taking the time to let us know how we're doing. We really appreciate hearing from you and hope you'll continue to let us make shopping "lighthearted!"

With warmest regards,

7.5   *Saying Thanks When It's Hard to Do*

Asked to address a convention, this employee was a flop—poorly organized, often lost, and a real bore. Still, his effort must be acknowledged. This letter tactfully thanks him without exaggerating his talents.

This letter is appropriate for a one-time effort that went wrong. If the reader must keep doing whatever he or she did so badly, you will want to follow your letter with face-to-face advice about improving performance.

Dear Sam,

We are grateful for the considerable time and expertise that went into your special presentation for our annual convention. It was greatly appreciated.

We can't hear your important message too often, and you gave our people much to think about in the months ahead. Your energy in the face of technical problems was admirable, especially in the difficult after-lunch time slot.

Accept our gratitude for your hard work and dedication. Thank you again, very much.

Best regards,

7.6　*Offering Congratulations on Published Article*

A short note like this one is all it takes to acknowledge a customer's or employee's accomplishment.

> Dear Gene,
>
> Your article in the December issue of the *G.A.S.P. Journal* was great. I'm not sure which I appreciated more—your insight into the problems of our industry or your lively writing style.
>
> Gene, all of us at G.A.S.P. owe a lot to you and the other members who take the time to keep our industry in the forefront. Thanks for contributing and being such an enthusiastic booster.
>
> Sincerely,
>
> P.S. Your ideas about exports were on target and tremendously helpful.

7.7　*Offering Congratulations on New Job*

When a customer changes jobs, offer best wishes in a note like this—and be sure to follow up in a month or two to see if your company's services are required.

> Dear Suzanne,
>
> I was delighted to read in the *Wall Street Journal* yesterday that you are now with the XYZ Corporation.
>
> What a triumph for them to get you! But they have a reputation for attracting the best people, and I'm confident you'll soon eclipse anything done by your celebrated predecessors.
>
> Congratulations!
>
> Cordially,

7.8   *Offering Congratulations on Promotion*

Acknowledging a promotion with a brief letter like this builds the customer relationship and makes it easier to talk about organizational changes that may affect your account.

> Dear Ruth,
>
> I just heard you've been promoted! Mazel tov, felicitations, and yahoo! Allied couldn't have made a better choice.
>
> It will be a pleasure to know our account is in such capable hands.
>
> Best wishes,

7.9   *Offering Congratulations on Award*

Any kind of personal accomplishment can be acknowledged—earning a new degree, having a child, getting married. A short note like this one is all you need to say in order to make your customer feel good.

> Dear John,
>
> Congratulations on being selected Volunteer of the Month in your community. I read about the award in the business pages and was very impressed by your commitment. I was proud to show the article to our staff and say—this is one of our best customers!
>
> Thanks for all you do, both for your community and for your loyalty as a customer. We appreciate the opportunity to help your business stay on top.
>
> Best regards,

Part II

Letters to Employees

Clarity is a key objective of all letters concerning human resources matters. Yet being clear is not enough. How things are said and how they are presented is also critical. Human resources matters can be sensitive and confidential—and saying the wrong thing in print might not be fixable with an apology.

That is why the *tone* of a letter is especially important in this area. Your tone should match your letter's message. A letter to a promising job candidate might aim to convey warmth, interest, and the sense that there could well be an opportunity to join the firm in the future. Conversely, in a warning letter to an employee, the tone would reflect the seriousness of the offense and make it clear that change is necessary and must be immediate.

Your letter's *voice* is also important. In many instances, passive voice is a better choice than active voice. While active voice can add color, vibrancy, and movement, in certain human resources communications active voice will sound harsh, cold, and accusatory.

For letters about sensitive issues, passive voice has a number of virtues. In active voice, the action is performed by the subject of the sentence. In passive, the subject is acted upon. This indirect construction is perfect for situations where tact and diplomacy are requisite. If you were an unqualified job candidate, which of the following letters would you prefer?

Active: *Dear Mr. Henderson:*

> *We have evaluated your application and concluded that your skills are inadequate for our opening.*

Or

Passive: *Dear Mr. Henderson:*

> *Your application has been carefully evaluated. Unfortunately, your qualifications do not meet the criteria established for this position.*

As you can see, the passive voice is ideal for softening the blow of bad news, presenting negative information, or placing the focus on the reader rather than the writer. It is also the right choice for communication that must be objective and impartial. Active voice can make communication seem biased.

Two Approaches to Organizing Letters: Direct and Indirect

How you organize the information in your correspondence will depend on what you have to say. In routine letters that are positive or neutral in tone, you will want to get right to the point. Here you would use a *direct* approach. In these cases you would state the most important fact at the beginning of your letter or memo, followed by any supporting details or explanations. This approach works well in situations where the news is good. Someone who has gone through a grueling series of interviews would appreciate being told she got the job at the letter's outset. The direct approach is also effective in instances where the correspondent doesn't ask the recipient to do anything, or requests something relatively easy such as completing a brief form and returning it in an envelope that has been provided.

When you have unpleasant news to relay, an *indirect* approach is a better way to present your information. Here, again, is where the passive voice comes in handy. With an indirect approach, you would first build a case, then conclude by revealing your decision or action to the reader. Let's say, for example, you have to tell employees their health insurance premiums are going to increase 15 percent in January. Rather than start out with this fact, which will most likely be met with groans and grumbles, you might begin by explaining you have had a larger percentage of claims this year than in previous years, as a result the insurance carrier has raised the company's rates, etc. As they read the letter, the employees will know what's coming. However, by presenting your case step-by-step, you have given them reasons to understand and accept the coming increase.

There are certain situations where the indirect approach should not be used to shield the reader. The shock value of the direct approach is more fitting and desirable. In correspondence relating to misconduct or other disciplinary matters, for example, information must be presented in a strong, direct, no-nonsense fashion.

Legal Ramifications of Letters to Employees*

Every time you write a letter to an employee or a potential employee, you risk saying something that may come back to haunt the company. The following statements illustrate just a few of the potential problems:

1. *As long as you continue to do well, you will always have a job with us.* This statement goes right to the core of the employment-at-will relationship. Courts have ruled that statements like this constitute an implied contract of employment. Once an implied contract exists, employment is no longer at will, and the employer is no longer free to terminate the employee with or without cause.

2. *Our situation does not mesh well with your personal needs.* This statement from a dismissal letter cost an employer more than $200,000. The employee being dismissed had returned to work following surgery for a malignant brain tumor. When he returned to work, he asked for and received approval to drop 20 percent of his work load, with a corresponding reduction in salary. Four months later, he was fired.

   Shortly before the employee's termination, he received a call from management encouraging him to work more hours. Then his employer sent him a dismissal letter that included the above sentence. This matter was settled by the employer agreeing to pay the ex-employee $200,000, to

---

* *Most of the information in this section was contributed by Wessels & Pautsch, P.C. Wessels & Pautsch is a law firm that exclusively represents management in labor and employment law matters. The firm maintains offices in St. Charles and Chicago, Illinois; Milwaukee, Wisconsin; and Davenport, Iowa.*

reinstate the employee in a new job, and to train company managers in the employment provisions of the *Americans with Disabilities Act.*

3. *Your salary will be $20,000 per year.* Courts have held that this statement implies an employment contract because the employee's salary was expressed as a yearly figure. To avoid this pitfall, quote salary in terms of a weekly or a monthly figure.

4. *You will receive a performance review every December.* This statement certainly seems innocuous. The danger lies in the company's failure to live up to the "promise" it contains. A better statement might be, "You will receive an annual performance review." This does not commit the company to reviewing the employee during a specific month and reduces the chance that a court will construe "every" to mean "every year into the future."

5. *You will be paid $10.00 per hour.* If this statement is made to an independent contractor, it may be interpreted as establishing an employer-employee relationship. Communications with independent contractors should be worded to strengthen, rather than call into question, the working relationship between the independent contractor and the firm. For example, payment should be by the job (not by the day, hour, or other measure of time) and should be described as "contract payment." Instead of "discharge," refer to "contract termination."

6. *Our medical review officer has indicated to us that you are at increased risk for back injury.* A statement like this in a follow-up letter to a job applicant who has taken a post-offer physical examination can cause serious problems for the company. The applicant who is denied a job solely on the basis of perceived "increased risk" of injury may well succeed in proving discrimination under the *Americans with Disabilities Act.* The ADA prohibits an employer from relying on increased risk of injury as a basis for its refusal to hire. The ADA mandates that the employer must look at whether the applicant is able to perform the duties of the job.

7. *We look forward to a long and prosperous future together.* What may appear to be no more than a pleasant way to close an offer letter could lead to major complications for the employer. Alluding to a "long future," according to the courts, creates an implied contract of employment, and consequently, eliminates an employment-at-will relationship.

8. *While you are on leave, the company will pay your health insurance premiums for you.* A company that wishes to extend this offer to a valued employee should be aware of the following legal pitfalls. The offer cannot be restricted only to valued employees. The company must be prepared

to make the same offer to all similarly situated employees, or risk the real likelihood of an employee lawsuit charging disparate treatment.

If the company offers to pay the employee's insurance premium, it should nevertheless provide the employee with a COBRA notice. Otherwise, the company may be sued for failure to furnish a COBRA notice and may find itself on the hook for sizeable medical bills.

As these examples show, imprecise or careless wording in business correspondence can do far more than confuse. It may also create binding contracts and other legal commitments that were not intended. A company may lose thousands of dollars as the result of these unintentional legal obligations, either in payment to employees who sue successfully or in legal fees as the company defends itself against the lawsuits.

Knowing that your letters may one day be presented as evidence in a courtroom, be particularly cautious of the things you commit to paper. The following employment writing checklist may help you avoid common errors that could translate into major headaches for you and your company.

Employment Writing Checklist*

This checklist illustrates some common pitfalls to avoid when writing on behalf of your company. It is not an exhaustive list of legal considerations, and various state laws may limit or void some of the ideas which follow. Please check your state's law before relying on any of these suggestions.

❏ Avoid terms of duration when describing employment, such as: *permanent* employee; salary of $35,000 *per year*; welcome to the [company name] *family*. This will help preserve your at-will relationship.

❏ Avoid terms like *probation* that would indicate a future dissolution of the employment-at-will relationship. Courts have indicated that this term can cause employees to reasonably believe that after they are off probation, they have gained security in their positions. Substitute *introductory period* and *orientation period*. For disciplinary actions, use *immediate and sustained improvement*.

* *This checklist was developed and contributed by Skip Sperry, Compliance Attorney with IEC Management Resource Group. IEC is a human resources consulting association based in Boise, Idaho. It serves over 800 employers throughout the Pacific Northwest.*

❏ Avoid unnecessarily binding your company with words like *must* and *will*. Substitute permissive language such as *may* or *might*.

❏ Avoid words of promise or guarantee. Rather than saying "Employees will have an *annual* review," substitute terms like *periodic, as warranted*, or *as needed*.

❏ Do not make inclusive lists, especially of disciplinary offenses. Explain that the list is illustrative, not exhaustive.

❏ Write only what you are committed to doing. Don't unknowingly place additional requirements on your company. For example, if it is not required by state law, do not include marital status in your equal employment opportunities statement unless your company wants to make that commitment.

❏ Use clear and concise language in your documents. Courts will construe ambiguous terms and conditions against the party who wrote the language.

  • Avoid using legalese, especially in documents that perform a quasi-legal function (policies dealing with EEO, affirmative action, etc.). The temptation to use legalese increases when you write about an area where compliance with the law is an issue, but try to stick to language that will be readily understood even by the untutored reader. If you must use certain legal terms, define them and relate them directly to your readers and the action they should take.

  • Use everyday language. Eliminate excess verbiage and avoid innuendo. In other words, say what you mean and say it in as few words as you can without omitting vital information.

❏ Find third parties to read your documents and tell you what they think the document indicates and implies.

❏ Include an appropriate at-will disclaimer in any documents that could conceivably be construed as promises or contracts. Place at-will disclaimers in prominent positions and ensure they are conspicuous (use bold type, larger typeface, etc.).

❏ When drafting documents that will be distributed to employees, indicate that the company reserves the right to modify, change, amend, supplement, rescind, or append the contents, but any changes must be in writing and signed by management. The documents cannot be changed orally by any employee.

❏ If the document is important and may have legal implications, consult your company's employment lawyer or association.

Chapter 8

Recruitment and Offer Letters

Letters to job applicants are among the most frequently written business letters and can be the most sensitive. The letters in this chapter cover every step in the employment process, from acknowledging a resume and scheduling an interview to turning down an applicant after several interviews. These sample letters use language that is clear but respectful—an essential ingredient of any letter to a job applicant.

The job applicant always deserves to be treated with courtesy. A letter that bluntly tells an unqualified applicant that he would never be offered a job with your company, even if it meant world peace, could needlessly damage the applicant's ego as well as your company's reputation. The inflammatory letter would, of course, enrage the applicant and justifiably. It would be safe to bet that he would eagerly and angrily tell others of this negative experience with your organization. The image of your company could be tarnished and may keep someone who would be an asset to you from considering your firm as a desirable place of employment.

Letters to candidates you wish to hire must also be carefully worded in order to maintain an employment-at-will relationship between you and the candidate. This legal concept allows the employer to hire and fire someone at any time, and the employee to quit and seek new employment at will. Except where a written agreement such as a union contract or an executive employment agreement is in force, most employees are considered employees at will. As a result, employers have the latitude they need to base employment decisions on economics, performance, and other factors.

The at-will concept can be accidentally compromised if your letters or your employee handbook make statements that a court can consider implied contractual obligations. As the section on legal ramifications of letters to employees makes clear, an innocent phrase like "we look forward to a long and prosperous future together" may be used against you in court by a disgruntled ex-employee.

By following the examples in letters 8.8, 8.9, and 8.10, you can confidently draft employment offer letters that tell your potential employee everything he or she needs to know *without* making promises that land you in hot water.

8.1   *Acknowledging Receipt of Resume in Response to Ad*

Always begin by thanking the applicant.

A short summary of the situation and the time frame will prevent calls from anxious applicants wondering about the next step.

Closing sentence is graceful, positive, and implies good things about the applicant without saying anything specific. An excellent choice for a form letter to many applicants.

Dear Ms. Banks:

Thank you very much for expressing an interest in the position of director for our Public Policies Affecting Children program. At present we are assessing resumes and during October will request interviews with those individuals who seem to combine strong public policy experience with a range of other skills. If we do seek a chance to speak with you in-depth, we will contact you within the next two weeks to determine your interests and availability to meet. Unfortunately, time will not permit us to see everyone who has contacted us.

Virtually every resume is a reminder of the number of committed and talented people interested in improving conditions in our city. We appreciate hearing from you.

Sincerely,

8.2   *Acknowledging Receipt of Unsolicited Resume*

Letter begins by thanking the applicant for writing.

This paragraph politely tells the candidate "Don't call us, we'll call you."

Passive voice softens the suggestion that the applicant may not be qualified for a position with the company.

A wish for the candidate's success ends this otherwise terse letter on an upbeat note.

Dear Mr. Perry:

Thank you for submitting your resume to Walden Pharmaceuticals for employment consideration.

An appropriate member of our employment staff will review your correspondence to determine if a suitable opening exists. Should you qualify for a currently open position, we will contact you promptly. If you do not hear from us, a position that matches your qualifications is not available at this time.

We appreciate your interest in our organization and wish you every success in your job search.

Sincerely,

8.3   *Acknowledging Receipt of Resume from Unqualified Candidate*

Instead of opening with a thank-you, this letter uses the direct approach and opens with the bad news.

Mentioning exactly what the museum is looking for prevents the reader from feeling unfairly treated.

Adding the first-person voice sounds more personal than a letter written strictly in the third person. This applicant knows someone really did read her letter and resume. Using only "we" might make the reader wonder whether anybody bothered to read it.

Dear Ms. Brewster:

I have received and reviewed your letter and resume. At the present time, we do not have an editorial opening and can offer you no future encouragement. Should such a position become available, we would be looking for someone with previous editorial experience and at least an M.A. in art history and/or English. Since your background is not an exact fit to our requirements, I would suggest you contact other area museums. Your qualifications may better match their criteria.

Thank you for your interest in the Woodstock Institute of Art, and the best of luck to you.

Sincerely,

8.4   *Informing Post-Interview Applicant That Company Is Still Deciding*

Don't keep candidates in suspense if your search is delayed! This letter is clear about what is happening so applicants know where they stand.

Offering a telephone number to call if there are problems is empowering; the process will seem less one-sided to the candidate.

As always, close the letter with thanks.

Dear Ms. Ellwood:

Thank you for your recent visit to Bristol Engineering.

While our search is progressing smoothly, its time frame has been longer than anticipated. Please know that we continue to consider you among our active candidates.

A decision regarding the position of engineering manager is expected within two weeks. We will contact you again at that time. If this delay presents a problem, please call us immediately at (800) 772-1895.

We appreciate your patience and your continued interest in Bristol Engineering.

Sincerely,

8.5   *Rejecting Applicant Without Interview*

Letter opens by thanking the candidate for applying.

Writer avoids saying anything discouraging about the applicant, but makes it clear no opportunity is available now. In ten years this person may be exactly the right candidate for a position—and how she is treated today will determine whether she bothers to apply.

Letter closes by wishing the applicant luck with her job search.

Dear Ms. Krammer:

Thank you for your recent inquiry advising us of your interest in pursuing a career with BBD Corporation.

We have reviewed your resume and samples from your portfolio. Unfortunately, we are unable to offer you further encouragement at this time. This is in no way a reflection upon your fine career development, but rather is due to our limited and very specific staffing requirements at this time.

Again, we appreciate your interest in BBD. We hope you will soon find the challenging and rewarding position you seek.

Sincerely,

8.6   *Rejecting Applicant After Interview*

After one or more interviews, it's appropriate to address the candidate by his first name.

This letter takes the indirect approach, delaying the bad news for the second paragraph.

Never reject anyone until your leading candidate has accepted the job. "The status of your candidacy is currently on hold" allows the company to make an offer if the other applicant turns down the job.

The last paragraph expresses personal sentiments and best wishes for the future.

Dear David:

Thanks again for your interest in career opportunities in the corporate communications department of Winston & Harrison, Ltd. We deeply appreciated the time and effort you expended during your recent visit. We were most impressed with your willingness to share your thoughts regarding your success at Devonshire.

David, as I indicated during our last conversation, the status of your candidacy is currently on hold. We have found an applicant who better meets our current needs, and in fact, have made a formal offer which from all indications will be accepted.

From a personal standpoint, I want you to know how much I would have enjoyed working with you. I am hopeful that our paths will cross again in the future. Until then, may I extend my very best wishes for your continued success.

Sincerely,

8.7 *Rejecting Applicant After Several Interviews*

Nothing is harder than turning down a candidate after several interviews, and in this case, after she and her husband have traveled some distance to visit the company and discuss relocating. Expectations are high and the candidate's disappointment is sure to be keen.

This bad news paragraph reassures the candidate of her worth but provides a solid reason for selecting another candidate—a reason that is directly tied to the duties of the job.

The company softens the blow by using passive voice to express its regret and acknowledge that the choice was difficult.

By promising to contact her about other positions, the writer keeps the door open for future possibilities.

Dear Pamela:

Thank you again for your continuing interest in Paxton Laboratories. We appreciate the time and effort you devoted to learning about career opportunities with our company. It was our pleasure to host you and Steve during your recent visit.

We have now completed the final phase of our recruitment process for the position of vice president, sales and marketing, and as promised, are notifying all candidates. Pam, we were most impressed with your educational credentials and work experience; however, we have decided to offer the position to another candidate whose background includes the management of a much larger sales force.

This decision was not an easy one. It is always distressing when there are two very well-qualified applicants and only one opening. It is regretful that we could not find a place for both of you.

As Paxton continues to grow, there will undoubtedly be other positions for which you could be considered. We will be in touch with you to determine your interest whenever such positions become available.

Best wishes for continued success.

Sincerely,

8.8   *Making Offer for Entry-Level Position*

A job-offer letter needs to be clear and precise—while avoiding phrases that might compromise employment-at-will status.

The first paragraph tells the good news right away. Salary is expressed monthly to preserve "at will" relationship. Both the employee and a court might interpret a yearly figure as an employment agreement.

Writer clarifies expectations and compensation for overtime.

By using "orientation period" instead of "probation period" the writer avoids implying that employment will be permanent after 90 days. "Approximately" gives the manager some leeway in scheduling the performance review.

"You have an exciting career before you" is better than a phrase such as "We look forward to a long and fruitful relationship" that may be interpreted as a promise of permanent employment.

Dear William:

I am delighted to offer you the position of management trainee. Your beginning salary will be $1,300 per month paid on a semi-monthly basis.

As we discussed, your position will require some mandatory overtime on an as-needed basis. You will be compensated for overtime hours that you work as statutory requirements provide. Including overtime, your monthly earnings will be approximately $1,650.

The first ninety days of employment are considered an orientation period for all employees. This provides Enterprise with a specific time to evaluate performance. At the end of thirty days or so you should expect to have a meeting with your manager to discuss your progress. A similar review will occur approximately ninety days after the start of your employment.

Training classes will be held throughout the summer. Please contact me at (214) 555-7444 no later than Friday, March 28, to schedule your classes. Also, if you prefer to live in a specific area, please be prepared to give us that preference when you call. We will make every effort to accommodate your preferences in light of our specific needs.

I look forward to hearing from you soon. Again, welcome to Enterprise. We think you have an exciting career before you.

Best regards,

8.9   *Making Offer for Middle-Management Position*

This letter uses bullets to clearly summarize the elements of the offer.

Salary is expressed in months rather than years to preserve employment-at-will relationship.

The next two paragraphs directly address the employment-at-will issue and ask the candidate to consent to employment-at-will by signing and returning the letter.

The closing is flattering and optimistic without making promises about the candidate's future at the company.

Dear Ms. Washington:

On behalf of Juno Manufacturing, I am pleased to extend our offer of employment as group leader, quality assurance. The specifics of the offer are outlined below:

- starting monthly salary of $3,800

- participation in QPC bonus plan

- participation in group insurance and leave benefit plans, as detailed in the current employee guidelines handbook and the enclosed brochure on our flexible compensation program

- three weeks paid vacation and 12 company holidays

This offer is contingent upon your signing all of our employment forms (including the receipt for the employee guidelines handbook) and agreeing to the concept of "employment at will."

This constitutes our entire employment offer to you, and any implied or verbal agreements or promises have no force or effect. This offer letter must be returned, postmarked no later than March 12, or the offer will be canceled. You may indicate your acceptance by returning the original letter, signed and dated, noting your reporting date of April 9. A copy of this letter is included for your records.

The selection process has been very rigorous, and we are pleased to offer you what we believe is an excellent opportunity. We look forward to your joining the Juno team and are confident you will contribute to its continued success.

Sincerely,

8.10   *Making Offer for Executive Position*

Using the direct approach, this letter opens with the good news and clarifies that it contains the company's formal offer of employment.

All the particulars of salary, bonus, and vacation are included so the candidate and the employer have a record of the offer.

Contingencies are also mentioned. Item three makes no promises about the length of time the employee may stay if her performance is unsatisfactory—an important point should a dismissal lead to litigation.

This paragraph asks the recipient to sign and return the original by a specified date.

Dear Ms. Daniels:

I am pleased to extend to you a formal offer of employment. This written offer sets forth the entire agreement between you and Hunter International. It supersedes all prior agreements and understandings, whether written or oral.

- Job title: vice-president, sales

- Base salary: $10,000 per month

- Bonus: eligible in January to participate in the executive bonus plan

- Vacation: three weeks plus an additional two weeks for personal business

- Immediate supervisor: Ms. Robin Wright, executive vice president, sales and marketing

The following is a list of the contingencies to your offer:

1. All employment forms must be agreed to and signed.

2. You will agree to a pre-employment physical and screening.

3. If, within the first year of service, your performance is considered unsatisfactory, the company will continue your employment for a reasonable period of time from the date you are notified.

If you agree to the terms listed here, please sign in the space below and return the original of this letter no later than 5:00 p.m. on October 29. We look forward to receiving your favorable reply.

Sincerely,

Chapter 9

Benefits and Compensation Letters

Everyone understands a paycheck—but throw in insurance, vacation time, pensions, profit-sharing plans, and 401Ks, and employees start scratching their heads. Follow these guidelines to make letters about benefits and compensation clear and comprehensible:

- Write to the level of your reader. Not every reader has a college or even a high school education. Those who speak English as a second language may find reading any letter a struggle.

- Use simple vocabulary and avoid jargon. Before you use an acronym, spell it out, for example: "Health Insurance Portability Act (HIPA)."

- Always include a telephone number and the name of a person the employee can contact to discuss benefits options in detail.

- Consider developing a series of brochures that clearly explain your health insurance policies, pension plans, and other benefits plans. Your cover letter can touch on the main points and refer the reader to specific pages for in-depth information.

- Develop good relationships with your legal counsel, tax advisors, and benefits and compensation professionals to make sure your benefits program and the letters it generates comply with the many laws that regulate this sensitive area.

- For really complicated topics like pension plans, a letter is simply not enough. Help employees understand their options by holding small-group meetings that walk employees through the paperwork and carefully explain choices and their consequences.

9.1   *Summary of Benefits for New Employee*

Letter begins by welcoming the new employee to the staff.

Writer states the subject of the letter in the second paragraph.

A contact is included in case the reader has questions.

Bullets and numbered lists organize information that would be overwhelming if included in a paragraph. Short, clear sentences are easy for employees at all levels to grasp.

Dear Ms. Kennedy:

Congratulations on your new position as creative director with Aberdeen Advertising. We are pleased to have such an accomplished professional joining our staff.

During the interviewing process you and your new manager probably had many discussions concerning salary. Benefits, however, may have been covered only briefly. This letter will highlight the benefits to which you are now entitled as an Aberdeen employee.

If after reviewing the letter you would like further details about any of the benefit programs, please don't hesitate to contact the benefits and employee relations manager at (207) 555-1100.

GROUP INSURANCE BENEFITS

1. Hospitalization/Medical/Dental
   - provided free for you and your eligible dependents
   - begins on the first of the month following your start date

2. Life Insurance/Accidental Death
   - $100,000 basic life insurance and $100,000 accidental death insurance provided for you at no cost
   - an additional $100,000 in coverage available for purchase by you at the cost of 24 cents per $1,000 per month.

PENSION/RETIREMENT SAVINGS PLANS

3. Pension Plan
   - you will be eligible after one year of employment

- when eligible, you will pay 1 percent of base salary up to social security base and 2 percent of salary above social security base

- your benefit upon retirement will be 1.75 percent times final average salary, times years of service, minus half of social security award

4. Retirement Savings Plan (401K)

- you will be eligible after one year of employment

- when eligible, you may contribute up to 6 percent of base salary and defer federal taxes

- the company matches the first 5 percent at 100 percent

SICK PAY/LONG-TERM DISABILITY

5. Sick Pay and Long-Term Disability Coverage

- you may receive two months' full salary for personal illness

- after two months off the job, you may receive an additional four months pay at 65 percent of base salary

- after six months off the job, you may receive 60 percent of salary as long as you are disabled, up to a maximum of $4,000 per month, in coordination with social security

MISCELLANEOUS

6. Relocation Expenses

- cost of transporting household goods paid in full by the company

- real estate commission to sell your home paid by the company

The enclosed brochure offers details about each of these programs. I urge you to set aside time to familiarize yourself with your benefits package.

Sincerely,

ENCL: brochure

Complicated subjects like retirement plans should be discussed at length in a fact sheet or brochure. Summarize key points here, and refer reader to an enclosure for more details.

9.2   *Leave of Absence*

This is a standard letter authorizing a leave of absence. If your company has 50 or more employees, your leave-of-absence policy must conform with the Family and Medical Leave Act. Contact the Department of Labor for advice as well as for forms required for a leave.

Dear Brenda:

Your request for a leave of absence has been approved effective October 21. Before taking the leave, however, you must use all your vacation. You may either take the time off or request a lump-sum payment for all the days you have earned.

During a leave of absence some privileges are safeguarded, while others are not. In your case, your seniority will be protected for the purposes of benefit accrual, but you will not earn benefits while on leave. Your present position cannot be held for you; should you wish to be considered for future openings, you will have to submit a new employment application.

Brenda, we appreciate your many contributions to the company during your five years with us. Should you have any questions concerning your leave, please give me a call or drop by.

All the best to you in your future enterprises.

Sincerely,

9.3 *Leave of Absence (Continuation of Medical Coverage)*

You must make the same offer to all similarly situated employees or risk an employee lawsuit charging disparate treatment. Check with your legal counsel before committing yourself on paper.

This letter clearly spells out the employee's responsibilities regarding her health insurance coverage while she is on leave. Even if your company offers to pay the employee's insurance premium, you should provide the employee with a COBRA notice. Otherwise you may be sued for failure to furnish a COBRA notice and find yourself on the hook for sizeable medical bills.

Dear Julie:

It is my understanding that your unpaid leave of absence will begin on September 1 and end October 31. During this time you may continue your medical coverage or allow it to lapse. Should you choose to keep your health benefits while you are away, you will be responsible for the full amount of the premiums.

Your cost will be $250.75, payable the last day of each month while you are on leave. Your first payment will be due September 30. If it is not received by that date, your coverage will be terminated. Should coverage lapse, you will have to wait the standard period of three months when you return to active employment before you are again eligible for health insurance benefits.

Please make your checks payable to Yardley Press and mail them to my attention at: 1 Wrigley Plaza, Merrill Springs, TX 41111.

If you have any questions, or if the circumstances regarding your leave status should change, please give me a call at (214) 555-7944.

Sincerely,

9.4   *Request for Short-Term Disability*

Follow this format when you must explain a benefit that involves a complicated procedure and plenty of paperwork.

First, describe the paperwork that is required in order to consider the employee's request. Number each item.

Next, briefly describe each document and how it is related to the approval process. Use bulleted or numbered lists to make the information easy to grasp.

Dear Richard:

We have received your letter asking to be placed on short-term disability (STD). We were very sorry to hear about your accident during your recent skiing trip to Steamboat Springs.

Before your request can be considered, the three enclosed forms must be completed:

1. *Short-Term Disability Application*

2. *Authorization to Use Compensated Time*

3. *Termination of Disability Leave*

A brief description of each document and an explanation of the STD approval process follows.

Short-Term Disability Application

Short-term disability cannot be granted until it has been formally requested. Completing the STD application is the first step in this process. The application has three sections, each to be completed by a different party:

- Section one should be filled out by you, the requestor, then signed where indicated.

- Section two is for your physician to complete. It is recommended that you hand deliver the application to your physician and then follow up with him or her to ensure that the necessary information has been provided.

- Section three will be completed by human resources.

The application, with the first two sections completed, should be returned to my attention within ten days of your receipt of the form.

Once your application is returned, it will be evaluated and approval will either be granted or denied. If your application is approved, your recovery will be monitored throughout the short-term disability period by a medical consulting firm. They will confer with your physician and review your records to determine the status of your condition. Please be sure to let your physician know someone from the consulting firm will be contacting him or her. If your physician does not discuss your case with the firm's representative, your benefits will be delayed.

Authorization to Use Compensated Time

This form authorizes payroll to apply any available compensated time to your time sheet while your STD application is being reviewed.

To receive a paycheck during this time, you will be required to use all your sick days. Once your available sick time has been exhausted, you may authorize use of any personal and/or vacation time you have remaining. Any personal or vacation time used *after* the initial 10-day waiting period will be reinstated once an approval is made. Personal and/or vacation time used *during* the initial waiting period will not be reinstated.

Termination of Disability Leave Form

This form indicates when you are able to return to work and should be completed at the end of your disability period. Your physician will complete the top half and you should complete the bottom half. It is important that you bring this form with you the day you return to work.

I am available if you need additional information or simply have questions regarding the forms or the STD procedure. You may reach me at (315) 555-2301.

Sincerely,

Include a contact in case the employee has additional questions.

9.5   *Summary of Benefits to Terminated Employee*

Opening paragraph describes the subject of the letter and how eligibility was determined.

Subheads make it easy to see the contents at a glance. Short descriptions are clear and to the point.

This section explains why an exception is being made to company policy.

All employees covered by a group plan must receive a COBRA notice.

Dear Alexa:

This letter will review the benefits to which you are entitled as a terminated employee of Resurrection Mental Health Associates. Your eligibility for the benefits was determined based on your date of hire (August 6, 1984) and the date of your separation from the company (October 21, 1995). A brief description of each benefit follows.

VACATION: At the time of your departure from the company, you had seven unused days and 13 additional days accrued. You will be compensated for these 20 days of earned vacation.

SEVERANCE: Because your position was eliminated, you are entitled to two weeks of severance for each full year of service as outlined in Resurrection's severance policy. You will, therefore, receive 22 weeks of compensation. This will be paid to you in a lump sum once you have signed and returned the severance agreement given to you on October 27.

DISCRETIONARY BONUS: Company policy states that any employee who leaves the company prior to the end of the year is ineligible for a discretionary bonus. Given the circumstances of your departure, however, the company has decided to compensate you for all objectives met from January through October.

LIFE INSURANCE: You may apply for an individual life insurance policy within 31 days after termination of your group life insurance. An application for conversion coverage is enclosed for your completion.

PENSION: You are fully vested in Resurrection's pension plan and are entitled to receive pension benefits beginning on the last day of the month following the month you turn 55. Please keep the organization apprised of your whereabouts so your future pension payments may be processed in a timely manner.

401K PLAN: The necessary forms to authorize a distribution from your 401K account are enclosed. Please complete the sections highlighted on the request for distribution form. To receive your account balance, you must also complete the enclosed addendum. Before filling out these forms, you may wish to speak with a tax professional.

HEALTH INSURANCE: You are eligible to continue your health insurance under the Consolidated Omnibus Budget Reconciliation

Act (COBRA) of 1985, or you have the right to obtain conversion coverage without providing proof of good health.

If you decide to enroll in COBRA, you have 60 days from the date your Resurrection coverage ends to inform Resurrection of your intention to continue or discontinue coverage. Information concerning this program is enclosed in this packet. You should contact me as soon as possible to let me know if you wish to continue in the health insurance program.

If you would prefer conversion coverage instead, you must apply in writing and pay the first premium to our insurance carrier within 31 days after your group coverage ends. The 31 days starts on the date your coverage actually ceases even if you are still eligible for benefits because you are totally disabled. A conversion form is enclosed should you select this option.

Includes a contact in case the employee has additional questions.

Should you have any questions regarding any of the benefits, don't hesitate to contact me. I may be reached at (513) 555-2217.

Sincerely,

ENCL: forms

9.6 *Eligibility for Retirement Plans (Current Employee)*

Opening paragraph states eligibility date and calls attention to the enclosure.

Paragraph offers clear instructions and a deadline.

Letter includes a contact in the event employees have questions about this complex topic.

Dear Ms. Whitfield:

We are pleased to inform you that effective January 1, you will be eligible to participate in the company's pension and retirement savings plans. A brochure which briefly highlights the two programs is enclosed. Should you wish more detailed information, please see your employee handbook.

If you wish to enroll in the programs, please complete the attached enrollment forms. The completed forms along with a document verifying your date of birth (as outlined on the reverse side of the pension form) should be returned in the envelope provided no later than December 10.

Participation in the programs is not mandatory. If you decide not to enroll at this time, simply complete the applicable refusal cards and return them by December 10.

Decisions regarding retirement are very important and should be given serious thought. We believe these two programs are among the most important in our benefit package. They offer each employee the chance to make his or her future more secure.

If you have any questions after reviewing the materials, please give me a call at (612) 555-3150. I will be happy to speak with you.

Sincerely,

ENCL: brochure, forms

9.7 *Eligibility for Pension Benefits (Retired Employee)*

Opening states eligibility date and calls attention to enclosures.

Dear Ms. Chen:

At the time of your retirement from Dickerson Law Resources you were not yet entitled to any pension benefits. As of March 1, you will become eligible to receive benefits in accordance with the company's pension plan. The accompanying retirement benefits summary sheet shows your pension amounts. The details of these benefits are outlined in the enclosed materials.

You may begin receiving pension benefits as early as the date indicated in the section titled "Early Pension Options," or you may choose to begin payments on the first day of any month following this date. In the latter case, benefits will be higher than the early pension amount, but less than the full benefit for which you become eligible at age 62. If you elect to defer your pension, it will be your responsibility to notify the company at least three months prior to the date you wish your pension to begin.

Once you have made a decision on your pension option, please complete and send back the appropriate forms. If you elect the early pension option, please return:

- the *Election Form for Immediate Pension Options*

- the *Withholding Certificate for Pension or Annuity Payments*

- a copy of your birth certificate (or other proof of age)

- the direct deposit form, if this method of payment is chosen

If you elect to defer the start of your pension until a later date, please return:

- the *Election Form for Deferred Pension Options*

- the *Survivor Income Beneficiary Designation* indicating your marital status and your election or waiver of survivor income during the deferral period

If we have not heard from you within 90 days from the date of this letter, we will assume you have decided to defer your pension benefit to age 62. If applicable, your pension will be reduced for survivor income coverage calculated from your date of retirement to the date your pension begins.

Once payments begin, you may not select another option.

To ensure the accuracy of our records, please keep us informed of any change of address. If you have any questions or require any clarification, please give me a call at (218) 555-7389.

Sincerely,

ENCL: benefits sheet, forms

Writer is clear about the steps the reader must take.

Forms are listed to make it easy for the reader to follow instructions.

A contact is provided to advise the reader about her options in this complicated area.

Reader's reply should be kept on file in case questions about her choice arise when she is 62.

9.8   *Pension Benefit (Lump-Sum Payment)*

Writer describes the situation in the first paragraph.

You must inform employees of the tax consequences of their choice. This letter summarizes the consequences but refers readers to an enclosure and urges them to consult a tax advisor.

Numbered instructions are easy to follow.

Includes a contact in case the reader has questions.

Dear Mr. Powell:

The Glen Oaks Savings and Loan pension plan provides a lump-sum payment in lieu of monthly payments if, at retirement, the lump-sum equivalent of the pension is less than $3,500. Since the actuarial equivalent of your pension is $3,257.19, you will receive a one-time lump-sum payment in accordance with the plan's provisions. This distribution represents the total value of your benefit entitlement.

As of January 1, 1993, lump-sum distributions from qualified pension plans are subject to a mandatory 20 percent withholding of federal income tax unless the *entire* distribution is rolled over into an IRA or other tax-deferred plan. An important notice is enclosed concerning the tax treatment of lump-sum distributions. Please read it carefully and consult a tax specialist before making a final decision regarding the treatment of your distribution.

If you choose to take payment of your distribution directly, return:

1. the signed copy of this letter

2. the W4-P form should you wish additional taxes withheld above the mandatory 20 percent

If you elect the rollover option, please return:

1. the signed copy of this letter

2. attachment A indicating your choice of institution to which 100 percent of your distribution should be sent

Regardless of the option you select, we will need a copy of a document that shows proof of your age.

If you have any questions concerning the distribution, how it was calculated, etc., please contact me at (314) 555-7619.

Sincerely,

ENCL: notice, forms

9.9   *Pension Benefit (Vested Terminated Employee)*

Opening paragraph highlights enclosures and encourages reader to consult a tax advisor before making her selection.

Bulleted list calls attention to enclosures. If something is missing, the reader will know right away.

Numbered items tell reader exactly which forms are required.

Employee's selection should be kept on file in case questions arise when she reaches retirement age.

Dear Janice:

As a vested terminated employee of Artemis International Travel, Inc., you are entitled to pension benefits. The attached summary sheet shows the dollar amount of your retirement benefits under the company's pension plan. There are a number of options you should consider carefully before making your final elections on how to receive your distribution. The decisions you make about your retirement income will affect the rest of your life. Given the great impact your choice will have on your present and future finances, we strongly urge you to seek advice from both legal and tax specialists.

The following materials are enclosed to help you decide how and when you wish to receive your benefit:

- an overview of options available under the pension plan

- a brochure discussing major issues to consider regarding your benefit

- details of your pension benefit election

- tax information

After you have studied the materials, you will need to decide how you would like your benefit paid. Prior to making any election, however, you must do the following:

1. Provide an original or certified copy of your birth certificate or other document that shows proof of your age. If you plan to select a joint-and-survivor form of payment, you will also need to submit proof of your spouse's or joint annuitant's age. These documents will be returned to you after our review.

2. Provide your completed election form, including:
   - any necessary spousal consent (if you are married and elect a form of payment that reduces the otherwise automatic survivor payments to be made to your spouse);
   - your elections regarding tax withholding.

Since the value of your pension benefit is less than $10,000, you may elect to receive your benefit now in the form of a lump-sum payment, or you may defer your benefit until the age (as early as 55) you

Letter is clear about the time frame involved in this process.

A contact is provided in case the reader has questions.

choose to retire. Whatever your choice, you must complete the enclosed pension benefit election form and return it within the next 60 days.

If you choose a monthly benefit to begin at a later date, you can always change your election provided the change is made before the monthly benefit starts. Once your benefit begins, your election cannot be changed.

If you are at least 55 and wish to start your benefit now, please let us know. It will take a few months from the date of your retirement (or the date you return your completed election form after termination of employment) until you receive any payments. However, your payments will be retroactive to the date your benefit was scheduled to begin.

Please be sure to let us know of any changes in your address and/or phone number. If you have any questions or need further information regarding your pension benefit, do not hesitate to call. I may be reached at (415) 555-9390.

Sincerely,

9.10　*Insurance Benefits (Retired Employee)*

Opening calls attention to enclosure.

Simple sentences explain what the reader should do next, and when.

Provides complete information about the plan administrator.

Includes a contact in case the reader has questions.

Dear Ms. Hollister:

Enclosed is your retiree benefits booklet, *Partners in Your Healthcare and Life Insurance Benefits.* It contains information regarding the medical, dental, and life insurance plans available to Omni Media Services retirees. It also includes the current year's rate information.

If you wish to enroll in any or all of the plans, please complete the retiree insurance election form and the beneficiary designation form. Both forms should be returned to our offices within 21 days following termination.

All insurance benefits (medical, dental, and life) will be administered by the Retiree Medical Administration at company headquarters. After your benefits become effective, please direct any questions or requests for claim forms to Juanita Sneed, the retiree benefits manager, at:

> Omni Media Services, Inc.
> Retiree Medical Administration—QBC 24
> 5 Wilhelm Plaza
> Garibaldi, CT 05511
> (800) 555-2101

The Garibaldi office is open Monday through Friday from 8:30 a.m. to 5:30 p.m., eastern standard time.

If you have any questions regarding the enrollment procedure or the booklet, feel free to contact me at (219) 555-7441.

Sincerely,

ENCL: booklet

9.11   *Survivor Benefit*

Follow this example and keep your condolences sincere but short, unless you can add a personal memory or observation about the deceased.

Letter informs the survivor of the situation in the second paragraph.

Gives clear instructions as well as a time frame for the next step.

Includes a contact in case the reader has questions.

Dear Mrs. Harper:

We are sorry to hear of your husband's death and extend our sincere sympathy.

At this time we would like to advise you of the survivor income benefit to which you are entitled under the terms of the McClain Company's pension plan. As your husband's survivor, you are eligible to receive an annual benefit of $930.24, payable for your lifetime in monthly amounts of $77.52. Your first check comes to $185.04 and covers the period from December 20 through February 28. It will be mailed to you during the last week of January.

Please complete the enclosed federal withholding tax form (W4-P). If you wish your checks deposited into your bank account, also fill out the attached direct-deposit form. As I mentioned when we spoke, there will be a one-month waiting period before the checks will be deposited automatically. A return envelope has been enclosed for your convenience.

In order to complete our files, we will need a copy of your husband's death certificate as well as a copy of a proof-of-age document for you (birth certificate, driver's license, etc.).

Once again, Mrs. Harper, let me extend our condolences. If you have any questions, don't hesitate to contact me at (123) 555-0028.

Sincerely,

Chapter 10

Reprimand and Warning Letters

Reprimand and warning letters written in response to employee performance or misconduct need to be carefully written—both to convey the seriousness of the situation to the employee and to prevent expensive litigation. In order to avoid giving an employee grounds for believing an employment action was taken because of his or her sex, race, age, etc., your letter needs to be very clear about the incidents that led the company to make the reprimand and very specific about how those incidents are related to the employee's responsibilities. As you compose your letters, remember they may become public records should an employment discrimination case be filed. Write them so that if they were shown to a judge, a jury, or a government investigator, they would be helpful and not cause your employer any concern.

These letters must always, *always* be accompanied by another set of notes or letters stored in the employee's file: complete documentation of all performance evaluations, employee disciplinary actions, and other unusual occurrences that may be filed for later use in justifying employment decisions and discipline.

These events should be chronicled for two reasons. First, and most obvious, people simply cannot remember everything that goes on from day to day. Second, in our litigious society there is a tendency for courts and governmental agencies to apply the principle of: "If it isn't in writing, it didn't happen."

During a person's term of employment, the company should document the following:

- specific instances of performance that does not meet expectations, such as failure to meet production levels or insubordination, and performance that exceeds expectations

- specific instances of rule or policy violations

- all scheduled employee appraisals or reviews

- any conversation between a supervisor and an employee regarding work performance and any disciplinary action taken in response

- dates and reasons (if provided by the employee) for lateness and absence

- conversations regarding injuries on the job, to be filed in the employee's workers' compensation file.

Letter 10.7 shows how to document problems in a letter to an employee's file. The following are additional guidelines for documenting employee misconduct:

- Document every disciplinary event and counseling session promptly, while events are fresh in mind. Handwritten, dated notes are acceptable. Write as complete a story as possible, providing exact dates, times, places, and conversations.

- Record job-related standards and behaviors, not subjective interpretations. For example, instead of noting such behavior as "chronic absenteeism," record facts: "absent four days during December." Speculation such as "He's probably been drinking again" should not be included in the file.

- Focus on major issues related to performance and/or conduct and ignore minor issues.

- Be sure to record the employee's side of the story during counseling or discipline sessions. This will document that the employee obtained a proper hearing and will ensure the employee's account does not change later.

- In final warnings and other major disciplinary actions, make sure the employee reads and signs or initials the written record of the infraction and disciplinary action taken. If possible, have a second managerial or supervisory representative present at the meeting with the employee.

- Avoid documentation that gives the appearance of building a case against an employee. It is best to let the record reflect an honest attempt to salvage the troubled employee. Otherwise, the employer may be propelled into court by an employee claiming retaliatory discharge or a predetermined decision to fire.

- Be careful to record similar violations in the same terminology. The employer needs to be able to show other employees were disciplined for similar offenses in a like manner. For example, when two employees are disciplined for refusing to perform a job, it would be unwise to describe one employee's behavior as "unsatisfactory performance" and the other employee's action as "insubordination." In this instance, it would be best to record "refused to perform" for both cases.

Finally, keep in mind that the facts of the particular employment situation dictate the proper means of expression. When in doubt, contact the company attorney!

10.1   *Reprimand for Violation of Drug Abuse Policy*

Writer documents what has happened so far before discussing consequences.

Consequences are clearly outlined and related to the company's policy. Even better, you could cite relevant passages in your employee handbook.

Dear Ms. Baxter:

You were required to submit to a random drug screening last week in compliance with our drug-free work force policy-implementation procedure. The analysis has been completed and the results indicate illegal substances were present in your system (a positive result).

Because this is your first violation of the drug policy, the company believes you should have the opportunity to correct your behavior. You will be allowed to continue your employment with Langley, Inc., provided you agree to the following terms:

1. You will be suspended from work for a period of five working days. During this time you will enroll in a rehabilitation program and begin meeting with a substance abuse counselor. You will not return to work until the counselor has made a recommendation and a negative drug test has been received.

(continued)

2. You must successfully complete the rehabilitation program for substance abuse. Information and referrals concerning local treatment facilities will be provided by the company's substance abuse coordinator.

3. Urinalysis screens will be conducted as part of your treatment program. Screening intervals will be designated by the company. Communication with your counselor will be continuous throughout your treatment.

4. Subsequent urinalysis screens will be performed to detect if illegal substances are still present in your system. Screening will be on a random basis within 30 days of completion of your treatment program, then on a quarterly basis thereafter for a period of one year.

5. Failure to successfully complete a rehabilitation program, or testing positive during or after the completion of a program, will result in the immediate termination of your employment. Employees must remain drug free during the course of their treatment. Any employee who fails to complete an assigned rehabilitation program and is subsequently terminated will not be given the option of voluntary resignation.

6. If you choose not to participate in a rehabilitation program, you will have the option to resign in lieu of termination.

We strive to provide all our employees with a safe, healthy, and pleasant working environment that is free of substance abuse. During these next crucial weeks and months, your complete support and compliance in this effort is expected.

If you have any questions concerning the conditions outlined, or would like to discuss your screening results, please feel free to contact me at (219) 555-2155.

Sincerely,

Letter closes by offering the opportunity to discuss the reprimand personally. Be sure to document any conversation that may take place.

10.2   *Sample "Firm but Fair" Warning Letter*

Use this letter when an employee is not cooperating and is dropping hints about filing a discrimination suit.

Letter includes some positive language about the employee's service and hopes for a resolution to these problems.

Don't make your list inclusive. "Some of the areas of our concern" implies that while the list is illustrative of the problems, it by no means documents every concern.

Close on a positive note and indicate the next step—in this case, an evaluation in 30 days.

Dear Joe:

Because of the seriousness of the matters we discussed relating to your evaluation, I want to put this in writing so there will be no misunderstandings later.

Joe, I want you to know we value the service you have given us. As I have told you, I strongly feel you can contribute greatly to the success of our company in the future. We want you to contribute and to be a part of it. However, a number of negative factors have developed that we absolutely must address.

My deep conviction, which I have expressed to you, is that no company can succeed if there is disharmony and lack of cooperation on its staff. Our company is no different than other companies in this regard. These job-related problems we have discussed simply must be remedied. Specifically, here are some of the areas of our concern:

[Insert description of job-related areas of concern.]

Joe, again I want to make clear that we want you to succeed with us and to be a valued part of our organization. However, I want to also make clear that these problems we have discussed must be corrected, or we will have no alternative but to terminate your employment. In line with our discussions, you and I will meet again after 30 days to evaluate the situation.

Sincerely,

10.3   *Sample "Firm but Fair" Second Warning Letter*

Letter reiterates past problems and steps taken to correct them.

Writer then lists more recent incidents that have caused concern.

As in this example, be firm, but don't make threats. Because a warning letter may someday become public, it should be written so that, if it were shown to a judge, a jury, or government investigator, it would not cause the employer any concern.

Dear Sally:

So there is no misunderstanding, we want to put in written form our deep concerns about your job performance. We have talked with you on numerous occasions in the past concerning various aspects of your unsatisfactory performance.

Sally, we want you to clearly understand that we have every hope you will become a satisfactory and valued employee at our company. We think you have the capacity for doing this. However, your job performance to date has simply been unsatisfactory and we cannot tolerate it further. To do so would be unfair to your fellow employees.

In reviewing the background, we note the following:

[Insert job-related details, including past discipline.]

Most recently, the following has occurred:

[Insert job-related details.]

Again, Sally, we want you to know we would like nothing more than for your work performance to improve and for you to have a long and fulfilling career with us. However, we will not tolerate this continued unsatisfactory performance. You must clearly understand that if there are repeated instances of such unsatisfactory job performance by you, we will have no alternative but to terminate your employment.

Sincerely,

10.4   *Performance Problems—First Warning*

The shock value of the direct approach is appropriate in letters concerning misconduct or disciplinary matters.

Information is presented in a strong, direct, no-nonsense fashion.

Seeing this in black-and-white for the first time is certain to rouse a strong reaction in the reader—and motivate her to improve her performance.

Subheads and numbered items make the required changes as clear as possible.

Dear Suzanne:

Since you began working in the customer service department, there have been a number of instances in which you have made mistakes. Some of these mistakes have been very serious in terms of the costs to the company. They have also had a negative impact on our customers.

Each time these mistakes have been made, I have brought them to your attention. We discussed what was done wrong and what you must do differently in the future. We have spent a great deal of time going over correct procedures and ensuring that you know how to follow them. At the end of every meeting you have agreed to follow the procedures and to change behavior as I have asked. Yet, you still continue to make many of the same mistakes over and over.

After thoroughly reviewing your performance, it appears to me that most of these mistakes are not due to a lack of knowledge regarding procedures. Instead, most have been mistakes in which you did not take the time to follow the procedures. This shows me that with more attention to detail, greater conscientiousness, and better organization, you are quite capable of performing these duties.

The seriousness of your performance problems has reached the point where I must inform you that you may be removed from this position if your performance does not improve dramatically and immediately. The following list details the specific behaviors that must be followed from now on. As you will see, we have discussed them all before and we will discuss them in detail again. I will give you whatever help, training, feedback, and assistance I can. You, however, must take responsibility for making the necessary changes.

Performance Changes—Specific Behaviors Required of Suzanne Briggs

Task-Specific Behaviors

1. Legibly write down orders received by phone and verify the information with the customer while he or she is still on the line. Pay particular attention to: (a) customer number, (b) correct drop-ship number, (c) purchase-order numbers.

(continued)

2. When you enter orders on the screen: (a) ALWAYS view the comment file, (b) ALWAYS confirm the quantity, description, and ship date on the screen against your actual order form, (c) verify special pricing and additional discounts.

Organizational Behaviors

1. Organize your desk so that all of the catalogues, order forms, phone message pads, telephone indexes, etc., are easily accessible.

2. Use your planner to organize your daily tasks, note the calls you need to make, record conversations or important points you need to remember. ALWAYS call back customers when you say you will.

3. When you are given an assignment, ask questions if you do not understand it thoroughly. Listen carefully to instructions.

Interpersonal Behaviors

1. Talk to customers in a more courteous and professional manner. Mirror how they speak to you.

2. Be flexible if conditions arise that may make it necessary for you to leave later for lunch or stay a bit after 5 p.m.

3. If a mistake has been made with a customer, display empathy. Convey that we will do whatever is necessary to make things right.

Letter outlines a process and a timetable for addressing performance problems.

I will continue to work with you for the next 30 days on these issues. At the end of that time period, or prior to that if needed, we will meet again formally and evaluate your performance. If you have not significantly improved by that time, or if there are indications before then that you are not making adequate effort or are unable to improve, I will need to take further action, including possible termination.

Positive language about the person's potential should encourage her to make these changes.

Suzanne, I believe you have a great deal of potential and are very capable of succeeding in this position. I would like to see you continue in the department. My intent in pointing out these problems is to help you, if you are willing, to turn around your performance. Please view this as an opportunity to become better and more successful at your job.

Sincerely,

10.5 *Performance Problems—Second Warning*

Letter begins by reviewing the events that led to this situation.

Specific examples of the performance problem are included in this paragraph.

Writer adds impact by using the employee's name. The steps being taken as well as the timetable should be clear.

For major disciplinary actions, it is important to have the employee indicate that he or she understands the warning by signing or initialing the letter so a copy can be placed in the employee's file.

Dear Leslie:

On August 23, you were given a warning concerning your performance. You had failed to follow procedures for inputting and checking inventories into the computer system. Since that warning approximately one year ago, you have continued to have performance problems. Specifically, you still have not been following correct procedures.

Attached is a list of open purchase orders from several months ago. You were asked to check these and ensure that they had been handled correctly. When I examined the purchase orders I found you had stamped them as input, but you had not actually entered them into the computer. Not only does this mean you stamped them out of sequence, but it also indicates you did not check them against the computer printout as procedures require.

Leslie, your performance must improve immediately. You are being placed on probation for the next 60 days. During that time you will be given every bit of help and assistance you request. I will do all I can to help you, but you must show improvement and have no further incidents of this kind. If the problem continues and you do not show the needed improvement, further action will be taken, including possible termination or relocation within the company.

Sincerely,

I have read and understand this warning. I have also received a copy for my records.

_____   _____
Signature   *Date*

10.6   *Performance Problems—Suspension*

Letter starts with a recap of the situation.

Dear Peter:

You received a written warning on September 22 regarding the quality of your work. You were told that your performance would be reviewed in 60 days. During that 60-day period your work was to be error free. Since that time you have had two additional work errors, one on November 10 and one on November 18. This is unacceptable work quality.

Writer clarifies the step being taken and what the employee can expect to happen next.

You are being suspended without pay for the remainder of today and the rest of this week. During this time we will evaluate whether or not you should continue to work for the company. You should also take this time to consider whether you feel you can work here and perform at an acceptable quality level.

If you are allowed to return on Monday, you will have to work for a minimum of 90 days with NO work errors. If you have another error within this period, you may be terminated. Further disciplinary action may also be taken if you have errors after the 90 days expire.

Peter, we would like you to succeed in this job. We will help in any way we can, but in the end it is up to you to change and to approach your work with greater care.

Sincerely,

Writer secures employee's signature in order to retain a copy of the letter in his or her file.

I have read and understand this warning. I have also received a copy for my records.

_____   _____

Signature   *Date*

10.7   *Letter to Employee's File*

It's a good idea to write a letter such as this summarizing the situation for the employee's file. Documentation of disciplinary action may help the company prove action was taken solely because of job performance.

The general allegation that he is "constantly making mistakes" is backed up with specific examples. Even better, document specific instances and dates, for example: "mistagged 10 dies on September 11."

Follow this example and document any meetings between you and the employee.

As supervisor of the extrusion department, I have been working closely with Victor Abbott in the last few months as he has been learning his new job in the die shop. From my observation of his work during this time, I noticed he was constantly making mistakes. These errors, in my opinion, should not have been made by anyone who has been doing this job longer than one month. The mistakes I speak of include:

- mounting the dies up wrong

- mistagging the dies

- not taking the dies out of the hot box

- not putting the dies in the hot box when he was supposed to

- taking an excessive amount of time to mount the dies

Such mistakes will hurt the quality and productivity of the extrusion department. In my mind, they are mistakes that cannot be tolerated.

On January 25, the department head asked me and another department supervisor to meet with him and Victor. The purpose of the meeting was to discuss the mistakes and how they could be corrected. Victor was very defensive during the meeting. We were trying to help him, but he appeared to take the attitude that we did not have the right to tell him about his mistakes. After the meeting I told the department head that since Victor seemed so unwilling to listen, I doubted he would be able to perform his duties in the die shop in a satisfactory manner.

Chapter 11

Layoff and Termination Letters

When an employee leaves or is terminated, your company should document the reason for the separation from employment. If the employee voluntarily left or quit a position, you may want to obtain a statement from the employee stating that the separation from employment was indeed voluntary.

If an employee is discharged, the potential is high for the discharged employee to file some sort of complaint against your company. Therefore, extreme caution must be taken to document carefully the circumstances surrounding the separation from employment. If an employee is terminated because of poor performance and/or rule violations, be sure to document

- the specific incidents giving rise to the employee's termination

- witnesses to the specific incidents giving rise to termination

- the specific exchange of conversation that occurred when the employee was notified of his or her termination and the persons present at this time

- statements made by others with knowledge of the events giving rise to termination

The following four samples will help you draft layoff and termination letters appropriate for a wide range of circumstances.

11.1   *Elimination of Position*

The indirect approach works best for a layoff letter. Although the reader surely knows what is coming, the writer softens the blow by stating the business reasons behind the decision.

To:	Sam Pearson
From:	Human Resources Manager
Re:	Elimination of Position

Over the past year the company has seen a dramatic change in its business. We have acquired new processes which have streamlined our plant and shortened the time it takes to make our products. We have also acquired new customers with different, often simpler, product lines than those we have manufactured in the past. Because of these changes, we no longer have the same staffing needs.

We have evaluated all of our positions and concluded that some are no longer necessary. The job you do is one in which we now find that we have too many people for the available work load. The work force in your area must be reduced by 20 people.

Throughout the letter, the writer uses language that is respectful and sympathetic: "the difficult task," "I regret to inform you," "to ease this difficult change," "to assist you with your transition," etc.

This has left us with the difficult task of deciding who we must lay off. We have assessed each individual in your job class in relation to their seniority and performance. I regret to inform you that your job is one of the 20 being eliminated. You will be laid off as of today.

To help ease this difficult change, and to assist you with your transition as you seek another job, we will provide the following resources:

Bulleted list lets the reader quickly grasp the elements of the separation package.

- severance pay in the amount of two weeks' regular wages

- payment for double your accrued vacation time

- a referral to Manderly Outplacement Center. This includes a four-hour job-search course and four hours of personal job-search counseling

- a letter of reference from your supervisor

- a $500 credit at the Technology Center good for any training classes you choose to take to better prepare you for another job

Additionally, you may apply for unemployment insurance at the state job-service office. A listing of locations in the area is attached. The amount of your benefit is dependent on your past earnings. We have informed the job-service office of this layoff, and one of the case managers will be glad to assist you in completing the required paperwork to obtain this benefit.

Should our situation change in the future and we find we need to hire additional workers, you and the others who have been laid off will be eligible for recall into a job for which you are qualified. Your application will remain on an active status for the next 12 months, and we will notify you of any openings. Should you be rehired, you would have your seniority reinstated after one year of service.

Sam, you have been a valued employee to our company and we truly regret the need for this action. We wish you the best of luck. Please let us know if there is anything else we can do to assist you during this transition.

Letter closes with a personal note of regret and best wishes for the future.

11.2   *Notice of Impending Termination*

Dear Ms. Dixon:

Unfortunately, you have failed to comply with the company's request that you return to work immediately. This request was made because your approved disability period ended more than one week ago.

The records of your physician and the consulting firm monitoring your treatment indicate that you are now well enough to return to work full-time. Since your continuing absence is without basis, you are directed to report for work on Monday, March 12. If you fail to report, we will consider your job abandoned and will terminate your employment at the close of business on Monday.

If you have any questions, or there is anything you wish to bring to our attention, please call me as soon as possible at (615) 555-2850.

Sincerely,

The direct approach lets the reader know the consequences of her actions and the likely outcome of her continued absence.

The writer gives the employee one last chance to contact the company and explain herself.

11.3   *Termination for Misconduct*

This letter uses the indirect approach to recap the sequence of events that have led to the decision announced in the last paragraph.

Dear Ms. Reid:

On July 22 we met to discuss the incidents in which you were involved while in the office last Friday, July 19. Specifically, you were seen drinking alcoholic beverages and sleeping on the job.

From our preliminary investigation we learned that these occurrences were witnessed by several people, including your manager and other workers in your department. All said you were drinking openly, became intoxicated, then later passed out at your desk. You are well aware that such conduct is unacceptable and violates company policy.

Following the July 22 meeting you were placed on suspension without pay until the events could be investigated further. The purpose of this letter is to inform you that the investigation is now complete.

Your history with the company, particularly during the past year, has been filled with episodes like this latest one. In the last nine months you have received four written warnings for unauthorized absenteeism, tardiness, and poor productivity. You have been given any number of opportunities to correct your behavior, but to date you have chosen not to do so.

Based on the evidence in this most recent case, and your numerous past violations of company policy, the decision has been made to terminate your employment effective immediately.

Sincerely,

11.4　*Termination for Violation of Drug Abuse Policy*

The direct approach tells the employee that he is being terminated and why.

Dear Mr. Marshall:

You have violated the drug and substance abuse policy of Taylor Temporary Services. Effective immediately, your employment is being terminated.

After observing your odd behavior yesterday, your supervisor began to suspect you were under the influence of drugs. You were immediately sent to an off-site facility for testing. The results of that test indicate there were high levels of illegal drugs in your bloodstream.

This paragraph makes it clear that the decision to terminate is an outcome of procedures explained in the company employee manual.

The company has communicated to all employees on numerous occasions that it will not tolerate the use of illegal drugs or the abuse of legal drugs and alcohol. The company policy is to terminate those who violate the policy.

Even under these circumstances terminated employees must be notified of COBRA benefits.

Human Resources is waiting to discuss your COBRA benefits with you. Please return your keycard and ID to HR and make an appointment to pick up your personal belongings.

Sincerely,

Part III

Letters to Suppliers, the Media, Government Officials, and Shareholders

Customers and employees are not the only constituencies that help build a successful business. The letters in this section will help you effectively communicate with

- suppliers who assist you in manufacturing products and providing services

- the media, whose coverage can show your company to its best advantage or trigger an expensive and damaging crisis

- government officials who craft laws and mandates that can enhance or impede your ability to make a profit

- shareholders whose stake in your company provides the capital for growth and expansion

Chapter 12

Letters to Suppliers

Letters to suppliers need to be clear, concise, and carefully written—because they can, in a court, become binding legal contracts. Before you send a letter to any supplier, review it carefully to make sure it says exactly what you want it to—no more and no less.

12.1 *Requesting a Bid*

A request for bids should state your company's needs very clearly. If your specifications are complex, consider writing a short cover letter like this one and summarizing specs on a separate sheet, using plenty of bullets and headings to help the reader grasp the details.

Letter clearly specifies the deadline.

The supplier is provided a contact to call with questions about the bid.

Dear Webb Masonry Services:

Winslow Management is requesting bids from masonry contractors to make repairs to the walls and parapets of four three-story, 32-unit apartment buildings in the Waterside neighborhood. In order to be considered for this work, your company needs to submit a bid for all work by May 1. You must also be fully licensed, bonded, and insured.

I know you will have to view the buildings before you can provide an estimate for the work. To set up an inspection, please call me at (312) 555-4421.

Your bid should be accompanied by proof of insurance and five references from previous clients. Address your bid to me no later than May 1.

I look forward to your response.

Sincerely,

12.2 *Rejecting a Bid*

Don't burn your bridges when you turn down a bid. This letter thanks the supplier for taking the time to prepare the bid, and tactfully cites reasons for choosing another company. Let suppliers know your decision as soon as possible to avoid stringing them along.

Dear Mr. Webb,

Thank you for submitting a bid for masonry repair work to our four buildings. I appreciate the time you took to inspect the buildings and the thoroughness of your bid.

However, we have decided to give the contract to Olson Masonry Contractors. While your price was attractive and your references were good, Olson's larger staff enables it to better accommodate our tight schedule.

We will be sure to keep your information on file and will consider Webb Masonry Services for masonry repair projects in the future.

Sincerely,

12.3 *Accepting a Bid*

When you award a contract, your cover letter should mention important details covered in the contract. This letter confirms the schedule, the payment agreement, and mentions the two parts of the project: walls and parapets.

Dear Mr. Webb,

Thank you for submitting a bid for masonry repair work to our four buildings. We were very impressed by the price and quality of your work, and your enthusiastic references clinched the sale.

As a result, we have decided to award our masonry repair contract to Webb Masonry Services. As we discussed, you are to commence work on May 15 and complete as-needed work by June 1. Work on the parapets should be coordinated with Bob Nelson of Nelson Roofing. Our goal is to complete the entire project by July 1.

Enclosed please find a check for $2,500. As our contract stipulates, you will receive an additional $4,000 upon completion of the wall repairs and $15,000 when the parapets have been rebuilt.

I look forward to working with you in the weeks to come.

Sincerely,

ENCL: check

12.4 *Complaining to Supplier (Basic Format)*

When it's your turn to complain to a supplier, brainstorm ideas on a sheet of paper or PC. Vent your anger. Then, after an appropriate breather, start again and write at the top of the page: "What I want to be different after the reader reads this letter." Go back to your angry pages and underline everything your reader needs to know to provide the result you want. Discard the rest. What's left is your first draft.

Subheads, numbered lists, and underlined passages make it easy for the supplier to grasp the problems.

Before you send your letter, ask yourself a few questions. How will your reader probably feel after reading your letter? Is your anger directed at the right person? Will the reader be more cooperative after getting your letter? Will your letter produce the results you want? Refine your letter until it is a tool for productive change.

Dear Mr. Jones:

I need to know immediately what you will do to prevent any recurrences of the problems we have been having with your [describe].

Problems

- [describe, including date and time if relevant]

- [describe, including date and time if relevant]

Background

[If applicable, offer history of problem or supports and proofs of any damages caused by this problem.]

What I Want You to Do

1. By [set a time and date] [describe exactly what you want to happen or stop happening and offer a suggestion for a temporary emergency solution].

2. [Ask reader to provide a permanent solution, perhaps through a change in procedures or a meeting with XYZ officials.]

3. By [date], report to me exactly what steps you have taken and what additional help we can offer to see that this never happens again.

I'm confident you'll come up with a practical solution. We are eager to work with you so this won't recur.

Sincerely,

12.5   *Complaining to Supplier*

Letter starts by requesting a response, then summarizes the problem.

If problems are extensive or highly technical, enclose details on a separate sheet.

Underlined heading and numbered list tell the supplier exactly what the writer wants to happen next.

Letter closes on a positive but realistic note and emphasizes how serious the writer is about having the problem resolved.

Dear Ms. Roy:

I need to know immediately what you will do to prevent the unacceptable rate of failures of your Z-2000 diodes. Our contract allows a tolerance of 2,000 hours with a failure rate of .05 percent, but the failure rate has averaged more than three times that for some shipments.

Problems: Jack Carson's data on failure rates is enclosed.

Background: We met with Arthur Jefferson, Stan Laurel, Eve Arden, and you at XYZ on November 4 and again on January 10 to try to resolve this problem. Our notes from that meeting are enclosed.

What I Want You To Do:

1. Immediately authorize return of our current stock of 8,000 gross of Z-2000 diodes for full credit. (Copies of invoices and purchase orders are enclosed.)

2. Immediately ship us 8,000 gross of Z-4000 diodes. We request that these be billed to us at the lower Z-2000 rate.

3. By February 15, let me know exactly what steps you have taken and what guarantees you are able to make that your Z-2000 diodes will meet specifications in the future.

I'm optimistic that you'll be able to resolve this. We are eager to work with you and XYZ, but this rate of failures is totally unacceptable.

Sincerely,

ENCL: notes, invoices, purchase orders

12.6   *Canceling a Contract*

The letter begins by stating intention to cancel.

A clear reason is given for the decision.

Closes with a positive note about the future.

Dear Ms. Limanowski:

This letter is to notify you of the cancellation of the agreement between St. Hilary Church and LXX Energy, Inc., dated October 1995.

As you know, Marlene, we have relied on you for many years to keep our gas bill low by purchasing spot-gas contracts from out-of-state energy companies. However, Zenith Gas has offered us a very attractive alternative that will let us acquire gas at an even better price. After closely examining both Zenith's proposal and your terms, we have decided to switch suppliers.

It has been a pleasure working with you the last few years, Marlene. I appreciate your work and hope we find ourselves working together again in the future.

Best wishes,

Chapter 13

Letters to the Media and Government Officials

The media and government are very important constituencies for the business correspondent. Laws passed in Washington, D.C., or your state capital may determine the success of your business, while media coverage can boost or sabotage your company's reputation.

In both cases, well-written letters *can* make a difference. A clear, concise letter to a legislator may help influence a vote on an issue that is near and dear to you. Likewise, a cogent letter to a newspaper can set straight a record that has been smudged—or praise coverage that is fair and factual.

When writing to government officials:

- Keep your letter brief—no more than a page or two.

- Address only one issue in order to guarantee that your letter goes to the right staff member.

- Stress your connection to the official, mentioning whether you live in his or her district, or have a plant or employees there. If you have met the official, contributed to the election campaign, or voted for him or her, be sure to mention it.

- Get right to the point. Let the official know what your concern is and what you would like the person to do about it.

- Demonstrate your knowledge of the official's past record—refer to his or her voting record and stand on issues; note what you consider praiseworthy as it relates to your concerns.

- Ask for the official's position or a copy of any bills you are concerned about.

- Keep copies of every letter you send and receive.

On the other hand:

- *Don't* apologize for writing or taking up the person's time. Your legislators are there to represent you.

- *Don't* try to impress the official with your importance or exaggerate your case. Legislators can see through these manipulative techniques.

- *Don't* hesitate to take a strong stand, but don't unleash your anger. *How* you say something can drown out *what* you say.

- *Don't* send a carbon copy or a preprinted postcard. It implies that the official is not as important as the person who received the original.

Above all, spell the official's name correctly and use the proper title. When you're writing to an official in the executive branch like the secretary of labor or an assistant secretary of agriculture, call his or her office first to confirm the proper form of address.

13.1 *Complimenting Media Coverage*

When you want to praise a newspaper or television station, follow this example and be specific about what you liked and single out individuals whose work you appreciate.

Dear Ms. Walters,

We are very pleased with the way the *Lake Star* covered the dedication of our new widget-processing facility in Lakewood. The photo of our plant is splendid, and your reporter, Della Garcia, accurately captured the town's excitement about the new plant.

We believe the entire Lakewood community will benefit from our capital investment. The income generated by our 120 new employees will cycle through every business in the area, substantially increasing Lakewood's prosperity. We look forward to making a difference in Lakewood, and we thank you for telling our story so well.

We look forward to assisting you in future stories.

Sincerely,

13.2 *Responding to Unfair Media Coverage*

This letter defends an industry against damaging conclusions made in an article concerning one irresponsible company's problems. It starts by stating the writer's reaction and then plunges into a list of industry practices the article has ignored.

Don't sling mud. This letter merely points out facts that contradict the impression left by the article.

Dear Editor:

Your special report on the widget industry left me speechless. Our industry complies with the most stringent environmental laws and regulations and is highly regarded for its progressive approach to labor relations. By highlighting abuses by a single plant that industry experts unanimously agree should be shut down, you have portrayed the widget industry as a callous monolith indifferent to the environment of its communities and the health of its citizens. Nothing could be further from the truth.

Hundreds of dedicated employees work hard to see that our company's 10 widget plants are operated cleanly and efficiently. They work closely with federal and state inspectors who visit regularly to make sure those plants meet emission standards. In addition, our industry is working to find new ways to eliminate particulates generated by our manufacturing processes. Sadly, the Shemp plant featured in your article has turned its back on industry efforts and lags far behind the other 192 widget plants in the United States in EPA compliance. Because the company's failure to upgrade its procedures is an embarrassment to our industry, the National Widget Association recently voted to rescind Shemp's membership.

I hope future articles about the Shemp plant will tell readers its sloppy approach to environmental issues is atypical and the widget industry as a whole is committed to instituting practices that protect our air and water.

Sincerely,

13.3   *Writing a Legislator*

When writing to a congressional representative, follow this example and open by explaining who you are and what you want the representative to do: vote yes, vote no, co-sponsor legislation, etc.

Justify your position in the middle paragraphs. Be sure to point out how your position benefits other companies, your industry, or the public in general. This letter points out how the proposed legislation would benefit all companies using the team approach.

Dear Senator Smith:

Allied strongly supports S.295, the Teamwork for Employees and Management Act. I am CEO of a midsize widget company employing 250 workers, all of whom reside in your district. As you know, widgets are an important industry in our area, and we are proud to be the leading manufacturer of widgets in our state.

The TEAM Act would accomplish exactly what it implies: it would allow employees and management to work cooperatively toward achieving better quality products and improved performance for everyone's benefit. At Allied we encourage employee involvement at all levels. We consider our employees valuable assets with much to contribute to our success. However, under current law, employee involvement could be considered illegal. This contradicts what we believe to be good business sense and results in a chilling effect on cooperation in the workplace. This outdated provision in the National Labor Relations Act is inappropriate for business operations in today's economy. I urge you to vote for the TEAM Act when it is brought before the Senate.

The TEAM Act would amend Section 8(a)(2) of the National Labor Relations Act (NLRA) to deregulate employee involvement. When the NLRA was passed in 1935, Section 8(a)(2) was included to prevent employers from establishing "sham unions" intended to circumvent collective bargaining. However, over the years, the Act has been interpreted very broadly to prevent much more. Any company that establishes work teams, quality circles, action committees, etc., and includes any management participation, potentially violates the NLRA. This seems ludicrous in light of the new demands placed on business by global competition.

There is a growing awareness that employees have much to contribute, and when they are given a voice, their involvement significantly enhances quality, productivity, and employee satisfaction. Employee involvement is the natural evolution of worker-management cooperation in today's marketplace.

The TEAM Act would protect legitimate employee involvement programs, preserve existing protections against deceptive, coercive employer practices, and allow workers to discuss issues involving terms and conditions of employment. The Act expressly stipulates

(continued)

Letter closes by repeating the request, with underlining to highlight it.

that collective bargaining agreements would not be affected by this legislation.

This Act in no way disturbs existing bargaining units or the collective bargaining process. Allied believes that this amendment will clarify the rules of the workplace for millions of employers and employees, and bring the American economy into the 21st century. Allied strongly supports its passage and I respectfully ask that you vote to pass S.295.

Sincerely,

13.4 *Writing a Governor*

Reserve letters such as this for issues that require the use of a governor's power or that can be handled most effectively by the governor's staff. If an issue can be settled by a lower level of government, find out who has jurisdiction and address your concerns to that branch.

Follow this example to tell the governor who you are, why you are writing, and what you want him or her to do.

The middle paragraphs justify the writer's position.

The request is repeated in the closing paragraph.

Dear Governor Smith:

As the owner-operator of a widget plant located in downstate Centerville, I urge you to veto Senate Bill 119, recently passed by the Illinois legislature over vociferous industry objections.

As you know, 27 percent of all widgets manufactured in the United States are made in our state. I am proud to say that my plant makes almost a third of those widgets. However, should SB119 become law, 217 Squaw County residents will lose their jobs and Illinois production of widgets will plummet because I will be forced to move my plant to Ohio.

SB119 will outlaw the use of 10 chemicals in our state, including zernum. Zernum is a key ingredient in the widget-making process, and we simply cannot build widgets without it. Because our plant stores zernum carefully and uses it under close supervision, we have never had a zernum spill. All professionals who work with zernum conduct regular drills and are prepared to implement emergency techniques in the unlikely case of a zernum spill or leak.

Our trade association's researchers are hard at work identifying new synthetic substances that can be used in place of zernum. We anticipate that we will be able to stop using zernum altogether in three years—but in the meantime, we must be permitted to use it in order to keep our plant open.

I urge you to veto this legislation and to request our legislature implement laws that work with, instead of against, our state's biggest industries in discouraging the use of dangerous chemicals.

Sincerely,

Chapter 14

Letters to Shareholders

Most letters to shareholders of publicly held companies break every rule set forth in this book. They are dry. Boring. Long. But these letters are deliberately flat because that's the way the Securities and Exchange Commission likes it. To protect consumers from unscrupulous profiteers, the SEC requires publicly held companies to balance all positive or promotional statements with statements that can seem downright negative. In fact, a company whose letters discussed potential rewards without disclosing potential risk would quickly receive a letter of warning from the SEC.

Even dry and boring letters have a role to play. From the moment you welcome a new shareholder, you begin to build a relationship with that shareholder. The stronger the relationship, the more likely you are to keep your shareholder for the long haul. Many financial experts believe that investing in shareholder retention can lower shareholder turnover and increase long-term loyalty—an important factor when you are trying to dissuade shareholders from cashing out because times are hard. People who have held your stock for

20 years are not likely to sell just because short-term prospects are bleak or they are in the mood to buy something different.

To provide a continuous stream of information and build shareholder pride and stability:

- Send letters with every quarterly statement or prospectus. SEC rules permit a letter to be rosy and upbeat provided it is accompanied by a prospectus that provides a balanced assessment of the company's fortunes.

- Convey a positive message with periodic newsletters. Try reprinting positive stories about your company, or interviews with industry experts who can paint your company as successful.

- Make a priority of answering letters and phone calls from shareholders. No one will feel loyal to a company that appears indifferent.

- Consider scheduling regular town meetings where shareholders can meet and discuss concerns about the direction of your company.

The three letters in this chapter provide a foundation on which to build a shareholder communications program. But before you put anything in the mail, have it reviewed by a qualified securities lawyer to make sure it complies with all SEC regulations.

14.1   *Welcome Letter to a New Shareholder*

Start off by welcoming new shareholders. To the SEC, a letter like this is innocuous. But add a statement like "the forecast for the remainder of this year is positive," and you will have to offset it with a warning phrase. Fortunately, including a prospectus can satisfy that requirement.

Dear Mr. Lavin:

As president and CEO of Manatee Aquatic Equipment, I would like to welcome you to our community of shareholders. I believe you have invested your money wisely, and I look forward to a long and profitable relationship with you.

My purpose in writing is to assure you that we share the same goal: the long-term growth and profitability of Manatee Aquatic Equipment. You will receive quarterly reports describing how we are reaching our goal, as well as invitations to our annual meetings. While I hope you can attend them—and I see by your address that it is a possibility—if you cannot, I urge you to participate in our decision-making process by exercising your proxy voting rights.

The writer lets the shareholder know his or her opinions are valued and the company will respond promptly to all inquiries and concerns.

If you have any questions or comments, don't hesitate to contact me. You will hear promptly from me or our shareholder relations staff.

Thank you again for joining the Manatee community.

Sincerely,

14.2   *Notification of Annual Meeting*

A legal notice of your annual meeting should follow this format. Include a proxy statement for the shareholder to sign and return if he or she cannot be present.

Notice of Annual Meeting of Stockholders

to Be Held June 12, 1999

To the Stockholders of
MANATEE AQUATIC EQUIPMENT, INCORPORATED:

The 1999 annual meeting of stockholders of Manatee Aquatic Equipment, Incorporated, will be held on Thursday, June 12, 1999, at 10:00 a.m., at the Schaumburg Holiday Inn, 721 Golf Road, Schaumburg, IL. The purposes of the meeting are

1. to elect a board of eight directors, each to hold office for one year or until a successor is chosen and qualified

2. to approve or disapprove the selection by the board of directors of Smith Smith Smith as independent auditors for the company for the year ending December 31, 1999

3. to transact such other business as may properly come before the meeting

Stockholders of record at the close of business on April 15, 1999, are entitled to notice of and to vote at the meeting.

By order of the board of directors,

Virgie Othello, President

If you cannot attend the meeting, please mark, date, sign, and return the accompanying proxy in the enclosed envelope.

14.3 *Cover Letter to Annual Report*

A cover letter like this can highlight accomplishments because it is accompanied by an annual report that contains a balanced and comprehensive picture of the company's fortunes.

Are you leaving computer mail-order after-market sales and pursuing a retail strategy instead? This is the place to tell your shareholders.

Dear Shareholder,

We are pleased to provide your 1997 annual report. We are very proud of the progress Manatee Aquatic Equipment has made in the past year, particularly the last two quarters of the year, and we are very positive about the prospects for 1998. Net earnings rose to $4.1 million or 32 cents per share in 1997 from a loss of $7.2 million or a loss of 55 cents per share in 1995. [If earnings were flat, say something like "While our recent quarterly earnings were disappointing, we remain optimistic about long-term prospects."]

[Highlight significant accomplishments of the past year—investments in state-of-the-art equipment, record-breaking sales, industry recognition, new executives, new store or office openings, etc.]

[Highlight new management practices or shifts in strategy that, while they may have some short-term cost, will benefit your company in the long run.]

While we have made significant progress in 1997, your board of directors expects the current management group to make even more significant strides in 1998. I am confident that by executing our current strategic initiatives, we will do just that.

Sincerely,